101
THINGS TO DO
WITH YOUR
PRIVATE LICENSE

LeRoy Cook

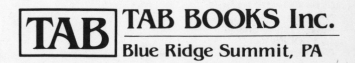

TAB BOOKS Inc.
Blue Ridge Summit, PA

To Dennis Shattuck, whose unfailing tolerance and support has meant so much throughout our association.

FIRST EDITION

FIFTH PRINTING

Printed in the United States of America

Library of Congress Cataloging in Publication Data

Cook, LeRoy.
    101 things to do with your private license.

    Includes index.
    1. Private flying. I. Title. II. Title: One
hundred and one things to do with your private
license.
TL721.4.C66   1985   629.132′5217   84-16442
ISBN 0-8306-2359-0 (pbk.)

TAB BOOKS Inc. offers software for sale. For information and a catalog, please contact TAB Software Department, Blue Ridge Summit, PA 17294-0850.

Questions regarding the content of this book should be addressed to:

    Reader Inquiry Branch
    TAB BOOKS Inc.
    Blue Ridge Summit, PA 17294-0214

Contents

Introduction

This is a book for young pilots—young in hours of flying experience, if not in age. When a new pilot finishes the course of training leading to his private pilot's license, he often enters a letdown phase, during which he wonders "What do I do now?" No longer carefully shepherded through each hour, he is suddenly left to seek his destiny unaided.

This book will attempt to pick up where student training left off, taking the new pilot on into areas only lightly touched in training—or perhaps omitted altogether. We will explore those first trips, enter unfamiliar airports, negotiate for FSS and ATC services, and learn to outsmart the weather. We'll talk about each of the flying seasons, from breezy spring to hazy summer, and on into foggy autumn and frigid winter.

Most importantly, we're going to discuss the pilot's need for understanding his limitations by developing the judgment and careful attitudes that will prevent a bad experience from turning into a tragedy. When and how to buy and fly that first airplane will be discussed, and we'll also talk about going on, taking advanced training for skills and licenses to be added to those of the basic private pilot certificate.

Learning to fly should continue throughout a pilot's career, an unending process more properly termed "learning about flying." When a beginning student asks "How long does it take to learn to fly?" I always employ my favorite rejoinder: "I don't know . . . I've never finished."

Each flight is a chance to learn more, and with all the wide and varied experiences available to the modern aviator there should be no reason to grow stale.

Come explore with us.

Part I
Striking Out on Your Own

Chapter 1
A License to Learn

It's a good feeling to have the private pilot checkride passed, to have all that dual and solo practice behind you. Now you're free to go out and just fly when and where you want, and with anybody you can talk into going along. Welcome, new pilot, to the real world of aviation.

Do you know what you've just acquired? A license to *learn*, that's what. Let's face it, you aren't a bit safer or smarter than you were before you passed your checkride, yet previously you couldn't have taken me for a ride, and now you can. The difference between then and now is that little slip of paper that says "Private Pilot" on it, and it means only that you've been tested and found free of unsafe gaps in skill and knowledge. You've got gaps all right, it's just that the government feels they are inconsequential enough to be filled in while you engage in your own personal flying.

Never, *ever*, stop learning about flying if you want to be around to give your grandchildren airplane rides and to eventually pass away of natural causes. There is so much to know I rather doubt that anyone can lay claim to all of it, yet you will look back on this moment years from now and truly realize how little you knew when you became a private pilot. You've been given all the training the average student can afford; the rest just has to come later.

The First Passengers

You've probably got a long list of people you have been promising to take for a ride, so call 'em up as the opportunity arises and share your joy. But, please, do aviation a favor and pick a good, quiet, still-air hour for their ride if they haven't been up before. Treat them gently; explain what you're doing so they won't jump and clutch when the wings bank and the sound of the engine changes. Keep the turns gentle and the climbs and descents shallow; don't try to prove your prowess as a fighter pilot.

Some people may seem reluctant to ride with you, a little afraid for their necks, perhaps, because they're being flown by a newly rated pilot. If they would only read the accident statistics, they would find that you're a safer bet now than you will be a couple hundred hours down the road. Right now you're still cautious and unsure of yourself. You'll ask for advice, you'll use your checklist, you'll pre-flight carefully. Sadly, all this tends to change when your logbook reaches the vicinity of the 200-hour mark. With a couple hundred hours of flying time, you're no longer a green hand, you're feeling like an old experienced pilot. You don't need those student pilot crutches anymore; you figure you've been around and seen it all. Most 200-hour pilots make it through this settling period, but some don't. The accident charts show a similar trend around the magic 1000-hour mark; "This is a lot of flying time," you'll think, "surely I know it all by now." Take it from me, *you don't*; I'm still learning just as much today as when I passed that thousandth hour.

Never Stop Getting Better

Now, where you go from here is up to you. You can fly the next 500 hours and gain 500 hours of experience, or you can log 500 hours and get one hour's experience repeated 500 times. Take your choice: Either learn from each hour and get better, or sit there insensitive and regress. Right now, you're probably thinking, "Heck, I'll bet some of the private pilots I know couldn't pass that flight test." You're right—they stopped learning the day they passed their checkride. They have never gone on to master 30-knot crosswinds or high-density traffic; they're right there where they were as student pilots. Resolve not to let this happen to you.

You told your instructor you would be back every little bit for some refresher training. Did you notice his half-smile? He's heard every pilot he graduated make that statement, and it almost never happens. Please, surprise him by coming back. As you will find out in two years, the biennial flight review does not constitute adequate refresher training. In keeping with your desire to learn all you can, get curious about something once in a while, and take an hour of dual to see what it's all about. Maybe you want to see inside a cloud, for real; get a CFI-I and try it—the right way. Maybe you want to see the world roll around this airplane; if so, take a sample aerobatic lesson. We all need a CFI to ride with us now and then, so find some excuse to make it interesting and you'll be more likely to do it.

Convinced that you want to get sharp? Good, just keep your eyes and ears open and fly—that's the way to begin. Now that you're a real pilot, take a short weekend cross-country or two. Just avoid a rigid schedule so the weather can't trap you, and have more than one destination in mind so you can outflank a front. Get out there and see how it really is. If you stay in the local area, hopping friends on a Sunday afternoon, you'll gradually lose your confidence and desire. Besides, someday you'll want to see another seacoast or the other side of the mountains, and you need to warm up first by making small trips before tackling a week-long journey.

Battling the Budget

Can't afford it, you say? Surprise, none of us can. Most of us do without something else to support a flying habit—things like lunch, golf, or a new car. If you can't fly as much as you want—and who can—at least hang around the airport and keep your antenna up, receiving the vibes. It'll keep you out of the bars, anyway, and that'll save money for flying later. Read all those flying magazines so you can benefit from the experiences of the other guys and gals; it'll all be helpful someday.

Thinking about buying an airplane? This is not the time; if you have the money available, somebody may sell you something you don't really need. You should rent the various types you're interested in, if possible, or maybe offer to pay expenses for an extended demonstration. Don't buy something because it's pretty, or after only one hop around the patch. Take it out and fly it cross-country an hour or two; that short jaunt may save you much more than it'll ever cost you. Go to a trusted FBO, CFI, or A & P, and ask him what he thinks; pay for his opinion if necessary, but don't buy an airplane in haste.

On the other hand, you might as well give up and buy something that isn't exactly perfect, as soon as you can make up your mind, just so you can maintain proficiency at your convenience. If you can make a good rental deal on a little-used airplane, fine and dandy, but after you are forced to cancel out a few trips and drive 200 miles in bright sunshine, you'll probably be an airplane sales prospect.

You might think weather is the great bugaboo of this business, and you'd be right. It turns up in the accident reports all too often, more than any other single factor, and it behooves you to hone and sharpen your weather sense. Whether you're flying or not, look up at the sky every day and analyze what you see there. Know what various types of clouds mean, which way good weather lies, and when a forecast isn't reliable. You must learn to be your own weatherman; don't abdicate this responsibility to others.

As time goes on, you will someday be looked upon as an old, knowledgeable pilot. Use the coming years and hours wisely so that this assessment will not be a mistaken one.

Chapter 2

Going Somewhere?

When you suddenly have a trip laid on to a place you've never heard of, getting organized to leap off in a hurry takes a bit of doing. Spreading out a chart and searching for an obscure destination leads only to fruitless frustration, and, likely as not, asking other pilots for a clue will provide the standard response, "Never heard of it." Fortunately, there is a better way to plan a flight, involving some diverse but successful methods.

Flight Planning

The term "flight planning" means looking over the route, laying out a course, and checking into fuel requirements and alternate airports. All of these assume that you know where you're heading, so if you don't, reach for the *Rand McNally Road Atlas* that ought to be in every flight case. No, we're not going to use it for navigation, but the *Atlas* does make it easy to locate an obscure town, so long as you know the state, by consulting an alphabetical index in the back of the book where each town is listed with its map coordinates. It beats the heck out of looking over a Sectional with a magnifying glass, only to find that the place you've been hunting was an inch beyond the edge of the chart.

Having used the Rand McNally to pin down this fishing spot, relatives' hometown, or sales prospect's plant site, note its approximate relationship to a large city (such as 40 miles south of Cincinnati on a major highway) and consult the appropriate Sectional Chart for the nearest airport. If you don't have the chart at hand, a diagram in the legend panel of every Sectional will tell you which chart covers the approximate area in question.

Choosing a destination airport is difficult with the meager information displayed on the chart, of course, making it wise to consult the *Airport/Facility Directory* for such details as runway composition, obstructions, hours of operation, and the like. Even more data is found, however, in the annually published *Airports, U.S.A.* directory from the Aircraft Owners and Pilots Association. The AOPA book compiles information on just about every airport in the U.S., cow pasture to major hub, including such choice tidbits as the brand of fuel sold, the operator's phone number, motel names and numbers, type of aircraft dealership—all kinds of good stuff. While the AOPA directory isn't the official word, being issued only once a year, it is helpful. Other airport directories are published, notably *Flight Guide* and *Jeppesen's J-Aid*, and various state aviation departments issue state directories, but most are limited in some fashion to keep down the size of the document, such as showing only data for paved airports or for those with runways over a specified length. Be sure your information is current; don't be above making a phone call if your airplane is going to require special services or runway dimensions. In the absence of such information, plan to have fuel in reserve to divert to an alternate airport.

Eyeball the Route

Now eyeball the route. If the trip is a long one, laying it out can take up the entire living room floor. And, because the Sectional Charts have two sides, it may not be possible to see all of a north-south route at once. For fast guesstimating, invest in a Flight Case Planning Chart, a 30-by-50-inch map that covers the whole U.S. at 60 miles to the inch. It shows each VOR station and the airways between, with mileages for each leg, making it mighty handy to see which airways take you where you want to go, as well as where practical fuel stops might be made. *Sky Prints*, a non-government VFR airways atlas, has been a cross-country standby for decades with revisions mailed monthly. Instrument pilots may use Jeppesen's low-altitude planning charts for similar purposes.

Long trips are perhaps most easily tackled on the VOR airways, where there is helpful course guidance preplotted and a guarantee of radio reception. But you may want to fly RNAV-direct by drawing a pencil line straight across the world; if so, break an extra-long flight into segments terminating in pit stops every two or three hours. Solo trips can be stretched out, of course, but don't abuse a passenger's endurance by optimistic flight planning. A yardstick or the straight edge of another chart will serve to rule off the course.

Check the route for hazards. You will wish to avoid busy traffic areas around major airports, military operations areas, and restricted areas. Also, look for sparsely-populated regions that have few airports; you want to alter your route slightly to stay closer to civilization. High terrain also may preclude a direct flight, if an airway would lead to your destination only by climbing to oxygen-required altitudes.

Always seek a route with good alternatives, in case you don't find ideal weather on your flight. It's wise to have two routes in mind, one for good VFR weather and one for marginal VFR use. If the weather goes sour, you may wish to abandon the VOR airway across trackless wasteland in favor of following a friendly highway or railroad that has towns and airports every few miles. IFR pilots should take a minute to consider a low-level alternate route also, in case it's necessary to go underneath the weather because of embedded thunderstorms or icing conditions. When flight conditions deteriorate, it's nice to be able to swing over to the preplanned alternate low weather route and press on, with a line of position under the wings and an alternate airport a few miles away at all times.

The old Rand McNally comes into play once again as a points-of-interest guide for the route. Part of flying's charm is the ability to look down on monuments, landmarks, and historical places; many of these are noted in the *Atlas*. It may be a business trip, but that doesn't mean you can't make a five-mile detour to see Monticello from the air. Naturally, you'll stay 2000 feet above the ground to avoid brushing the groundlings' sensibilities.

Writing It Down

For pity's sake, write down some of this hard-won information as you dig it out. Your flight log form may consist of a yellow legal pad, which is fine if you can make it do what you want, but you should have mileages, headings, and frequencies listed in order of use, with appropriate remarks such as "High terrain ahead" or "Watch for Harper's Ferry to left." Having mileages premeasured helps calculate "Howgozit" estimates in flight, when headwinds cut into fuel supplies or an unexpected tailwind tempts you to skip a stop.

If you're the type who hates to waste time, even while cruising crosscountry, play around with plotting aircraft performance. You can time decents and climbs, calculate TAS, groundspeeds, ETAs, and fuel burns from various tanks, all in the interest of learning more about your airplane's capabilities. Or your tastes may run to meteorology, keeping track of temperature lapse rates, frontal zones encountered, and indulging in pressure-pattern flying for optimum block speeds. Perhaps aerial photography intrigues you. The reason I mention these diversions in a discourse on flight planning is that I invariably forget about the camera or calculator—or even a spare pencil—until I'm airborne, so put them in the flight case *now*, before the balloon goes up.

Getting Organized in a Hurry

You won't always have the chance to indulge in elaborate flight planning. As a charter pilot, I have often made departures within 30 minutes after the phone call, but there is always time for *some* preplanning. At least take a minute to mark and measure the route, something which is next to impossible in the confines of the cockpit. If you're getting off VFR with a possibility of running into IFR weather, find the logical points at which to plug into the system for a clearance. You can always jot down times-over and figure estimates later, on the face of the chart if need be, but do your basic plotting down on terra firma, where five minutes' work can be time well spent.

Now assemble your flight planning goodies in a ditty bag or whatever, so it will all leave the house with you when you might not have full command of your faculties. You needn't tote a 40-pound flight case, just a clipboard and a couple of pencils in a plastic pouch, but it's awfully embarrassing to reach for a chart and find it was the one that slipped under the table last night.

As a final flight planning tip, take along an RON kit even on one-day flights. Having the toothbrush along ensures that you will probably get home tonight; the first time you forgot to carry your kit will be the day the forecasts go sour and you'll have to stay out with no razor or spare socks. An RON kit is like a good luck charm—as any charter pilot knows.

As the old saw goes, "Plan your flight and fly your plan." It's still good advice to follow.

Chapter 3

Efficient Flight Planning

Would you like to fly more and pay less? No, I'm not advocating a switch to an ultralight vehicle, I'm talking about getting more efficiency from your regular bird. Most of us have let poor flight planning and sloppy cruise-control technique become a habit. With the increased costs of avgas, we need to investigate every possible means of trimming our fuel consumption figures. It isn't necessary to scrutinize the upperair charts or invest in complex engine analyzers to do this, either. A few simple steps will stretch your fuel budget to cover 10 to 20 percent more mileage.

Fly More and Pay Less

Start by renewing your acquaintance with the airplane's Pilot's Operating Handbook. Every airplane/powerplant combination has a most efficient power setting for each flight condition, and you should no longer be content to use one set of numbers for all conditions. Suppose, for instance, you're just out tooling around the local area with some friends. Why blast about at 75 percent power, with the attendant noise and dollar drain, when you're really not going anywhere? A 60 percent setting will serve just as well, and in larger airplanes you may want to cut back to 50 percent or so. By doing so, you'll be saving fuel for the days when you really *are* in a hurry.

Finding the Airplane's Best Altitudes

A few general facts will become evident after reviewing the cruise charts. First, significant savings will result from using 60 or 65 percent power settings rather than 70 or 75 percent. For example, a Cardinal RG at 7500 feet will cruise at 169 mph on 74 percent power, burning 10.6 gallons per hour. Yet at 60 percent power it will still do 155 mph and use only 8.7 gph. By giving up 14 mph, one saves nearly

2 gph; the miles-per-gallon went from 15.9 to 17.8. Second, it pays to fly high. The Cardinal RG gives 149 mph on 60 percent power at 2500 feet, but 159 mph can be had on the same 60 percent at 10,000 feet. That's 10 mph extra without any increase in cruise fuel flow.

Now, we all know it isn't practical to cruise at 10,000 feet on every hop, even if weather conditions would permit it. It takes time and fuel to get up there, so the tradeoff must become advantageous before it will pay to go high. The fuel required to take the Cardinal RG from 5000 feet to 10,000 feet amounts to two gallons; therefore, a flight duration of more than two hours would be required to save enough fuel to warrant the extra climb. As a rule of thumb, you can usually afford to climb as high as 5000 feet above the starting point on trips of 100 miles, and as high as 10,000 feet for 200-mile hops.

A turbocharger will allow even higher and more efficient flight if your flights are long enough and you don't mind wearing an oxygen mask. Climb rates will remain brisk instead of tapering off above 10,000 feet, and fuel flow remains constant while cruising faster in the thin air. There's no such thing as a free lunch, though, and the cost and upkeep of a turbo, as well as its inherent slight increase in fuel burn, must be weighed against the number of high-altitude trips you will be making.

A bit of preflight calculation can be well worth the time, using the information gleaned from the winds aloft forecasts. In general, the winds aloft turn more westerly and increase in strength as altitude increases, making it natural to fly eastbound legs high and westbound trips low. But there are a lot of tricks up Mother Nature's sleeve, and you will find days when normal rules don't apply. Few trips are exactly upwind or downwind, so it's important to do some calculations to see how much effect you're going to get at various altitudes. Learn to choose the flight level that helps most or hinders least.

Learning to Lean

Oddly enough, there are still pilots flying who use the mixture control only for killing the engine after parking. Perhaps if it were colored money-green and had a dollar sign painted on it they'd take more notice. We all know the primary reason for having a mixture control in airplanes is to provide the best fuel/air ratio at higher altitudes. Yet it's a plain fact that fuel runs through the pipes slower as the knob is pulled further out, and because gas costs money, you can save as long as you lean without damaging the engine. The surest way to lean the mixture is by investing a couple hundred dollars in an exhaust gas temperature gauge. In less than a year the device will pay for itself, and maintenance is usually limited to occasional replacement of the probe in the exhaust stack.

Leaning with the EGT gives a reference point, or peak temperature of the exhaust, so you know when you're getting too lean for the engine's health. While some engines may be run at the peak EGT at low cruise, even leaning to 25° to 50° on the rich side of peak still saves plenty. Without an EGT, you can only lean cautiously until engine roughness first appears, then enrich the mixture until the engine runs smoothly again. Most likely, you'll then shove the mixture forward another quarter-inch or so to keep the valves cool, and vow once again to buy an EGT so you'll know what you're doing.

A Direct Route

Seeking out the airplane's best-mpg setting, choosing favorable cruise altitude, and learning to lean are just starters. There are many other money-saving measures available to the cross-country pilot. When possible, fly a direct route with no doglegs. The poorman's RNAV (area navigation) is still a pencil line drawn with a yardstick, and it works just fine. A ten-mile saving here and there adds up to a free trip every so often, so make an effort to straighten out your cross-countries. If you stick to that straight line, you'll be dollars ahead.

Climb, Cruise, and Letdown

An efficient departure requires that you become established in an on-course climb as soon as possible. Request the preferred direction from the control tower as you report ready for takeoff, not after liftoff. At non-controlled airports you should conform to the normal flow of traffic, but you can save time by making your departure from a tight traffic pattern rather than a leisurely meander over a five-mile circle. If you're departing in a direction opposite that of takeoff, make the turn back to the downwind leg as if you were remaining in the pattern, staying within a mile or so of the field. Then simply exit the pattern by climbing out the top and make any changes in heading after safely clearing the local traffic.

Since your best efficiency lies at high altitudes, it would pay to climb as rapidly as possible to the cruising level. Unfortunately, best rate-of-climb speeds tend to produce nose-high pitch attitudes that are uncomfortable for the passengers and block forward visibility. It's wise to seek a deck angle that lets you keep the horizon in view, even if it takes an extra minute or two to reach cruising altitude.

Airplanes with fixed-pitch propellers may suffer very little by climbing at an airspeed greater than V_y, because the increased rpm of a higher airspeed generates more horsepower, which translates into more climb. Full throttle is commonly used during climb in these aircraft, as the propeller pitch chosen by the manufacturer is usually best suited to cruise rather than climb, which limits the rpm available at low speeds. Airplanes with constant-speed props are more often than not climbed at reduced power settings to reduce the noise and wear of full-power operation. Some leaning may also be permitted in a reduced-power climb. However, climb power should be as high as practical for the most efficient climb to altitude; a minimum of 75 percent power would be recommended. Remember to advance the throttle to maintain desired manifold pressure as altitude increases until reaching the limit of throttle travel—usually 5000 feet or so at climb power settings.

Unfortunately, ideal cruising altitudes are not always available, due to weather or the limitations imposed by air traffic control if flying IFR. Any ice accumulated by climbing into a cloud deck can nullify the gain in efficiency—another reason to stay VFR. On the other hand, smooth air can provide 5 to 10 mph more true airspeed at the same power settings, making a climb to get on top of the rough stuff quite advantageous.

As you see your first checkpoint come into view, double-check your exact relative position. When fuel was cheap, it mattered little if one got a few miles off course now and then. It costs a lot more to get back on course at today's prices, so try to stop those deviations before they exceed a half-mile. If you're south of that little town when you're supposed to be north of it, make a slight heading change to return to the pencil line now, not farther along in the flight after you're off course five miles downwind. When flying by the VOR, back up the CDI needle with your plotted courseline; at long distances from the station there can be considerable difference in where your VOR needle says you should be and where you want to be. Fly the courseline, not the needle.

Now do some planning for the arrival before you actually get to your destination. It takes several minutes to let down from high altitudes, particularly if your passengers are new to light airplanes and must be descended at sedate rates. Plan a 500-fpm descent at cruising airspeed and project where you should begin letting down to arrive at traffic pattern altitude just as you reach the airport. You may be surprised to learn that a descent from 10,000 feet may need to begin 30 miles out. No doubt the greatest efficiency would be realized by shutting the engine down at cruise altitude and dead-sticking the last few miles, but that's a bit extreme, even at today's cost of operation.

The best method for perfecting your cross-country technique is to experiment on a route you fly regularly, keeping a log of your fuel consumption over the various trips. You may soon discover there's free flying available if you're willing to use your head.

Chapter 4

The Flying Vacation

You deserve it. You've been working like a Trojan for months. You're sick of getting up in the morning to face the same old rat race, and besides, the wife and kids want a vacation somewhere, too. This is as good a time as any to take off and get away from it all, to forget the mess at home and soak up new sights in unfamiliar surroundings. And since you're a pilot with a magic carpet at your disposal, why not make it a flying getaway, just like in the sales brochures?

What to Take Along

Before you start fitting a station wagon load of equipment into the airplane, some aerial vacation planning might be in order. Right away you must face the hurdles of space and weight limitations; you must reassess your baggage load in terms of the airplane's capability. You have probably been flying most of your cross-country flights with only a change of clothes and a toothbrush. This time you may be gone for weeks, and you must choose wisely to make maximum use of the available room.

Naturally, if you're used to traveling by any method, you will know enough to pick easy-care clothes, wash-and-wear items that will stretch your suitcase-full. A winter vacation will require extra weight and space allowance for the bulky coats and sweaters of the season. Summer flying, on the other hand, can mean doing battle with high density altitudes, another valid reason for careful weight and balance planning. If you're flying a four-place airplane, figure on using only three adult seats, or limiting the fuel load, to permit hauling vacation bags. Also, vacationing airplanes have a way of coming home with extra goodies stashed aboard, so don't load right up to gross when shoving off.

Most likely you will be required to set the date of your departure some time in advance, vacation schedules being what they are. Since you don't know exactly what the weather situation may be months or weeks ahead, have several routes to pick from. In case you can't get to Reno, try for Las Vegas. Anyplace is better than sitting around home waiting for the weather to clear. This is the secret of enjoying a flying vacation: Maximize the airplane's advantage—a rapid change of scenery—without locking yourself into a rigid schedule.

An evening departure after work can be a perfect way to start a flying vacation, depending on the weather pattern. It should be possible to fly several hundred miles before the evening gets too far advanced, in pleasant flying conditions. Stop short of extensive night flying, especially in unfamiliar country. But, with Daylight Savings Time spread over much of the year, that still leaves two or three hours for a getaway in broad daylight.

Accumulate the trip's baggage well in advance of zero hour, perhaps loading the airplane partially the night before, so something doesn't get overlooked at the last minute. Separate occasionally needed items, such as a hair dryer or travel iron, from RON essentials like shaving kits or makeup bags. Normally, if you pack correctly, only one bag per person will need to be hauled to and from the motel at overnight stops. Place inflight requirements, like munchable foods and games for the kids, in a separate box for the cabin. Keep cameras and film in their own bag, so you won't miss a shot because they were inadvertently buried in the baggage hold.

Carry some emergency gear on board, such as a set of jumper cables to help get going again after you leave the master switch on, as well as a spare airplane key wired somewhere under the cowling. Whether or not to carry a full-blown survival kit will depend somewhat on the terrain you are to cover and the time of year, but it's always a good idea to be ready to walk out of anything you intend to fly over. Drinking water is the most-overlooked item in survival gear; square plastic jugs are light and pack easily.

A cheap set of air mattresses and blankets, or even a light tent, are good items to have along if space permits, just in case you are forced to RON with no accommodations available. The floor of the pilot's lounge becomes much less foreboding with an inflated mattress and a warm blanket. A can of insect repellent can also make life in the wild more bearable, even if you hadn't planned on living next to nature on your trip.

Emergency aerial latrine facilities are better to have and not use than vice-versa. Handy commercially available containers can be had from pilot supply houses, or you can simply toss in an empty milk carton or a coffee can with a snap-on lid. Anything will look good in a pinch; just don't pretend the need for such items will never come up.

Chewing gum and earplugs make traveling much more pleasant, and some Dramamine should be kept on hand for the *mal du air* that an afternoon ride in the back seat can induce, along with sick-sacks for the ultimate bad scene. Keep everyone busy and entertained and the time will fly by uneventfully.

Take extra cash or traveler's checks along, as well as the basic credit cards, since you may run into things such as a tire that needs replacement, and you may not have the desired credit card match.

Shoving Off

When engaging in that enjoyable pastime of pretrip planning, don't overestimate your passengers' flying endurance; it's a rare crew that can withstand a three-hour nonstop flight. Make your hops an hour and a half or so in length, stopping for a stretch even if the airplane is still amply fueled. Everyone will enjoy the trip more, and you'd be surprised at the interesting stops that just happen to be found about 200 miles apart.

For the best riding conditions, try to make the long flights during the morning hours, before the midday thermals and surface winds start kicking up turbulence. Sightsee during the remainder of the day, and perhaps make a short late-afternoon flight to the next stop, after the vertical air movement has subsided. Don't plan on flying all day to keep a rigid schedule, unless everybody is a seasoned traveler. Not only will you have to endure some turbulence to keep up the pace, you'll be likely to encounter some vastly different weather systems on a long day's journey and you may not be able to reach the planned destination.

Keep It Flexible

By flying only half-days you will keep the schedule flexible, and you can always switch to afternoon flying to make up for a fogged-in morning without disrupting the entire trip. Naturally, leave several extra days unplanned for the inevitable weather delays or perhaps for lingering at a scenic spot that's just too beautiful to leave. Insofar as possible, make no firm dates in advance; you call for motel space when you get into town, and if everything is booked up, fly 50 miles down the road to RON. A fully planned itinerary, on the other hand, will mean countless long-distance phone calls to reshuffle the schedule when delays occur. As cheap insurance, file a flight plan while gallivanting around the country on vacation.

Don't figure on making every stop you have planned. Always lay out more than you expect to cover, so you'll have plenty of other places to go when one spot turns out to be dull. An airplane is a magic carpet, waiting to whisk you to a different world only a few hours away, without all the tedium of endless hours on the turnpike or in airline terminals. There's something to be found everywhere, and if you are forced to stop at an unplanned airport, ask around for the local attractions.

To keep ground transportation costs to a minimum, try to find a motel with airport pickup service near the scene of the first day's action, and use a rental car for the following day, rather than keeping it parked idly. See if public transportation or courtesy cars are available before dialing up a cab. Flying vacationers should wear old walking shoes to make up for their wheel-less state when grounded.

When negotiating new country, ask local aviator types about preferred routes and areas to avoid. Maybe a pass that looks good on the chart isn't too easy to negotiate when seen firsthand, or perhaps one lakeshore will offer better landing facilities than the other. If weather seems to behave differently than it does back home, get the opinion of the old-timer loafing in front of the line shack. It doesn't hurt to have all the help you can get, and you can reciprocate by helping strangers at your own airport.

Lightplane vacationing is easy, safe, and fun when properly undertaken. Don't expect your first trip to be like the same excursion in an automobile or on an airliner; just accept the benefits of general aviation and plan around its limitations. You'll have a grand time that will keep you fired up for next year.

Chapter 5

Low-Level Flying

Pilots generally equate altitude with safety, and rightly so. Altitude is like money in the bank that can be drawn upon for such things as regaining lost airspeed, pulling out of a goofed-up aerobatic maneuver, or increasing gliding range in the event of a forced landing. Even in smooth air, my usual minimum is 1,500 feet above the terrain—high enough to clear most obstructions and adequate for crossing small towns without a detour. This would let me reach an emergency landing spot up to two miles away, or one mile with enough altitude for a traffic pattern.

When You're Forced to Fly Low

However, there are times when you just can't fly as high as you would like and must sacrifice some of your altitude if you are to continue the flight. A VFR-only pilot must stay out of the lowering clouds along his route, as an example. Quite often a precipitation ceiling with light rain will reduce inflight visibilty to less than a mile when flying near the cloud base. Dropping down 500 feet or so can restore visibility to several miles—enough to find an airport and land. Clear weather with strong winds aloft is another challenge; it's not uncommon to find headwinds of 40 to 50 knots of 3,000 feet above the surface and only half that near the ground. The only way to maintain a reasonable groundspeed is to seek the lighter winds down low, which is perfectly safe if the terrain is not mountainous. Low-level flying does have some peculiar hazards, however, and we trust the old-timer won't laugh too much if we give some of his tips on what was once considered everyday flying technique.

How Low Can You Go

There are limits on how low you can fly. The FARs say to

Fig. 5-1. There are times when flying low is the only way to go. At the legal minimum of 500 feet AGL, one must take care to avoid houses, such as this one hidden in the trees, out of consideration for the noise impact on residents.

maintain sufficient altitude to negotiate a forced landing without undue hazard to persons or property on the surface, a "sufficient" amount evidently being left to the pilot's judgment. The regulations do require at least 500 feet above ground level outside congested areas, which is plenty low enough. I prefer to hold my low-level emergency flying to 800 feet in deference to any airport traffic patterns I might encounter. Detour airports, whatever their size, rather than bore straight through the traffic pattern at low altitude. Using a normal traffic pattern altitude also has benefits if a forced landing becomes necessary, since the approach legs will begin at a normal height. Keep a watch for rising terrain elevations on the chart, and update your altimeter setting whenever possible; you've little margin for error here. If you're sneaking along under lowering weather, set yourself some definite altitude minimums for a 180° turn. If you are forced to drop down from 1000 feet AGL to 800 feet or so, start planning a course of action right then, and when pushed down any further, get out without hesitation. The ceiling may be coming right on down, and you need time to find an airport. If you wait until 500 feet becomes 400, then 300, it may be too late to do anything other than risk a landing in the first pasture you can find.

Navigation

The most noticeable change from everyday flying will be the navigation techniques. Your range of vision is much shorter at low altitude, and checkpoints are difficult to spot until they suddenly appear under the wings. A highway intersection, for instance, lies hidden behind bordering trees or hillsides, and if you miss it by a mile you may never see it. At low levels the apparent groundspeed is much faster, which means a checkpoint will be gone from view in a fraction of the time usually available for identification. Don't be afraid to circle the landmark in doubt for a closer study; note the heading you were following before you started the turn, however.

Rather than blundering along half-lost, you'll soon find it becomes much easier to follow a well-marked highway or railroad that happens to be going in your general direction. Never mind the jokes about the "concrete compass" or the "iron beam;" at least you'll know where you are. I do suggest following such a route just to right of center—both for a good view of the roadway and to minimize chances of a head-on collision with someone following it in the other direction.

In areas where there isn't anything on the ground to follow, one falls back on dead-reckoning by clock and compass. To avoid getting hopelessly off course, note prominent landmarks—such as towns,

Fig. 5-2. Down on the deck, due to weather or strong headwinds aloft, this Citabria pilot sticks to open country and watches for obstructions.

lakes, roads or rivers—that lie along the route a few miles from the courseline. Then, if you find yourself over one of these points, it will be readily evident that you need to alter your heading to get back to the direct course. This is, quite simply, bracketing yourself so you catch the error before it gets out of hand.

What happened to the radio all this time? As you no doubt recall, the VHF frequencies are subject to line-of-sight limitations, and the signals can be blocked by high ground and curvature of the Earth at low altitudes. Over flat country you can get a course needle indication for 50 or 60 miles from the station, but beware if the to-from flag is not pulled into view. Such weak signals are not always accurate and should not be relied upon for precise determination of position. The ADF, bless it, is still usable even at ground level, as long as thunderstorms don't create false bearings. For the most part, you are on your own when cruising down on the deck, and you cannot rely on electronic guidance from the VOR.

Dangers to Avoid

Now, there is the matter of obstructions. Low-level flying would be fun if it weren't for the continuing proliferation of nearly invisible towers across the land. They pop up without warning as you fly along in the middle of the countryside—lighted and painted to be sure, but still mighty hard to see. Don't expect the Sectional Chart to keep you out of trouble. It may take a year for a tower to make it onto the chart, even if you fly with up-to-date charts. You can find revisions to the Sectionals in the Notices to Airmen section of the *Airman's Information Manual*, if you care to plot those tedious coordinates and mark towers under construction.

I had to learn about towers the hard way, so listen and learn: I was hired to deliver a man to a lakeside airport early one fall morning. We left at sunup, under CAVU skies, but as we neared the lake country a solid blanket of fog appeared. This wasn't unusual for the area, so I simply continued on a dead-reckoning course above the white blanket, watching for a hole in the vicinity of the airport. Alas, no holes appeared, and I wandered around for a few minutes, trying to give the appearance of doing all I could to get my passenger to his destination before giving up. I had already told him we were going back home when I spotted a lone hole with a certain marina's name painted on a boatdock roof. Instantly I was oriented; the airport was only a few miles down the road from the marina.

We spiraled down through the hole, finding a few hundred feet of murky airspace underneath the lifting stratus, and roared off down the highway to the airport. Sighting a windsock above the trees, I pulled off the power, coasted around a low, tight traffic pattern, and deplaned my shaken passenger after what I thought was a superb job of flying.

A local pilot strolled up and said, "Pretty low, isn't it? Watcha do, make an ADF letdown on the radio station?" He glanced down the highway in the direction I had come, and there stood a splendid example of the steelworker's art, poking up into the ceiling. Had I chosen to follow the road along the north side instead of the south side, I would have hit that tower dead-on. It was there on the chart, but who looks at charts when watching for an airport? I mumbled something about ADF to the man and slunk away, suddenly much older and wiser.

Therefore, plan a low-level flight as if you were heading into mountainous terrain, checking all along the route for maximum elevations to be cleared before choosing an altitude for flight. Don't let your eyes leave the windshield for more than a second or two, just in case an uncharted new obstruction looms into view. Fast airplanes are particularly hard to manage down on the deck, and it is only good sense to back off a little from max cruise in these birds, to give yourself more time to dodge.

When flying in canyons or valleys, be alert for electrical transmission lines strung across from rim to rim. Some states are requiring these lines to be marked with lights and orange globes, but most are noticeable only by their supporting towers. Don't try to go under the wires, judging height by the towers or poles; a long span always sways very low at the center, making successful attempts pure luck. And, just in case you've forgot, remember the cardinal rule of terrain flying: Never fly *up* a narrow canyon, always *down*, toward lower ground. The merging forks of stream beds will point the way downhill, if in doubt.

As a participant in many Civil Air Patrol search missions, I can testify that low altitude flying isn't for kicks; it's a hard, demanding job. Use it wisely, however, and learn its pitfalls, and it might bring you home someday.

Chapter 6

Dodging Tall Towers

As the sun's light scatters in the dense haze, the pilot peers into the milkiness through a windshield long since rendered semi-opaque by impacted insects. The visibility is reported to be three miles at the surface, but at an altitude of 1000 feet AGL it's anybody's guess. He checks the sweat-stained chart on his knees for the hundredth time, trying to match the chart's symbols with a village or turnpike in the circle of restricted visibility beneath the aircraft.

He isn't ready to consider himself lost, of course; few people will be honest enough to admit such a plight until it's too late for effective action. But it's been quite a while since he's felt that satisfied glow that comes with a solid fix.

Glancing up, the pilot catches the blur of a rapidly approaching image, all too close, at 12 o'clock level; it's a *tower*, a tall spike of slender steel suspended by a far-flung spider web of cables—and it's uncomfortably near. He cranks in aileron and elevator to escape the intruder's clutches and the top of the structure slides by off the right wing, a hundred yards away but still a near-brush with tragedy. Shaken, the pilot climbs an extra thousand feet to guard against encroachment on his airspace, but in doing so sacrifices still more ground contact to the all-encompassing haze.

We've all been that pilot at some time or another—a little off course, in poor visibility conditions, and a tad too low in an attempt to orient ourselves. Sometimes the pilot isn't so lucky and the tower snares the unwary aviator. It isn't just haze that can bring us down into the reach of obstructions; a low stratus deck over rising terrain can tempt a "gotta get there" individual into ducking under. Freezing temperatures at higher altitudes can dictate a low-level route, or the pilot may be letting down for a landing while still a few miles from the airport so he'll have time to slow down for the pattern.

Fig. 6-1. The tower just ahead of the wingtip measures 1444' AGL, but it isn't the only one around. Barely visible in the center of the picture, right of the curve in the road, is a 1626-footer some five miles away, and two smaller towers may be seen near the bottom center of the picture.

Preflight Precautions

Whatever the reason, recognize the potential for disaster when you enter a thicket of steel near the ground and take steps to minimize the danger. It would be easy to say you'll never fly lower than 1000 feet AGL, the breakpoint between large and small obstruction symbols on the Sectional Chart. However, that's no guide to safe operation in itself. The tall-tower symbol only warns of an obstruction *taller* than 1000 feet; it doesn't say it can't be 2000 feet tall, as in the case of the towers just off the airway east of Springfield, Missouri. Also, it's easy to overlook an elevated bit of terrain decorated by a relatively small 500-foot tower, but that combination of hilltop and steel spike are enough to bring the top of the tower into frequently used airspace. Be sure to judge terrain elevation by the ridges, not the valleys.

Of course, Sectional Charts have large numbers in the middle of each lat-long grid, signifying an altitude increment that will clear the highest known object in that block by 100 feet or more. A "12," for instance, calls for a minimum flight altitude of 1200 feet MSL, which could mean an obstruction as tall as 1099 feet MSL could be found in that particular grid. Because altimeters can be as much as 70 feet out of tolerance, this leaves scant room for error.

For protection without constant checking, the Sectional's title block carries a warning of the highest known terrain or obstruction, but this advice is largely wasted in western states, because one side of the map may depict terrain 10,000 feet higher than the other side, where the warning would have little significance. The Jeppesen or NOS low altitude enroute charts also provide some obstruction-height warnings, as MEAs on the airway structure will give an obstruction clearance of at least 1000 feet along the airway. Approach plates bear one or more MSAs (minimum safe altitudes) for the maneuvering area, generally valid for a 25-mile radius of the final approach fix.

Keeping Watch Inflight

Well-known metropolitan towers may seem to present less hazard than the countryside's crop, but in reality any safety advantage will probably be negated by the thicker traffic density around the city antenna farm, even though its location is very well known. However, one simply doesn't expect to encounter a 1200-foot needle out in the vacant spaces, where the pastoral scene lulls pilots into lethargy. The guy wires will normally reach out 80 percent of the tower's height from the base, so a 2000-footer will have wires

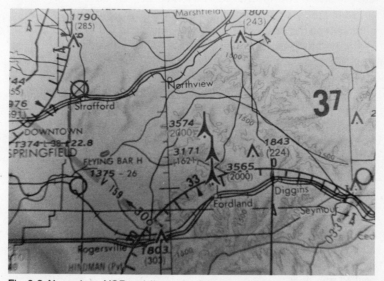

Fig. 6-2. Near a busy VOR and airway, here are two 2000-foot towers, plus a third one measuring a mere 1621 feet tall! Note the "37" on the chart, calling for a minimum of 3700 feet of altitude in an area of 1500-foot terrain elevations.

spanning nearly five-eighths of a mile, even more reason to give tall towers a wide berth wherever they are encountered.

Free-standing microwave towers are more easily spotted than guyed towers, due to their heavier structure; they tend to be shorter as well, although there is an 1163-foot free-standing TV tower just off the end of runway 18 at Kansas City's Downtown airport. Haze can make even thin guyed towers stand out in relief against a white background, as opposed to the ground clutter that camouflages them on a clear day. Even so, the snowblind pilot flying in haze might not see the steady-state approach of a tower with his name on it. It's the ones that don't change relative position that get you, so take a peek behind the window posts periodically.

You generally should not fly at low altitudes at night, but towers are easier to spot in the open countryside during hours of darkness. However, they are sometimes camouflaged in well-lit city areas. Dawn or dusk is the worst time for spotting landmarks, of course, towers included, particularly if one is looking into the sun.

Placement of towers is certainly not done without restriction; proposals for construction near airports must meet clearance-slope guidelines issued by the FAA, which has final authority over structures higher than 199 feet AGL. Towers shorter than 200 feet need not be marked or lighted. If you see a notice of proposed construction posted on the local airport bulletin board, check it out in relation to your area's arrival and departure patterns; you may want to comment on the proposal in order to shift the tower to a less critical spot. It's much harder to get a tower decommissioned or moved once it's built.

In Summation

Include a check for obstruction clearance in your preflight planning, noting safe altitudes on your flight log in advance of takeoff. Keep a Sectional Chart handy during all off-airways flights. Don't fly with enroute charts only. Don't take it for granted that everything is charted; remember there's a lag of six months or longer between commissioning and updating. Few obstructions will protrude more than 2500 feet above the mean terrain, so stick to higher altitudes whenever possible. If forced to fly right down on the deck, plan on foregoing idle conversation with passengers and devote your full attention to the approaching scenery. There's no way an airplane is going to win an encounter with a steel tower, so plan on never challenging one.

26

Chapter 7

The VFR Flight Plan

Remember the VFR flight plan, that hoary anachronism from student training days? Have you called one in to Flight Service lately? Probably not, because most pilots seldom think about the chances of being forced down short of their destination. The fact is, there's still a place for the VFR flight plan as a free trip-insurance policy that pays off big if your rubber band breaks somewhere enroute.

Flying cross-country used to be a bit more challenging than it is today. Flight plans were quite popular, because if trouble cropped up, it was just a matter of time before someone would come looking for you, and the flight plan told them when and where to start. Airplanes were slower, airports were less plentiful, and lightplanes often were not equipped with radios, so once airborne, there was no way to check one's bearings or get a weather report. The flight plan was vital for added peace of mind.

Times Have Changed

With improved equipment, times have changed. Nearly all aircraft have a radio or two, and we generally have good inflight communications during the entire course of the flight. We may even be able to get a friendly ATC controller to give us flight-following service by radar. As the term "flight-following" was used originally, it referred to a type of VFR flight plan that assumed that you would check in at each VOR along your route, and FSS personnel would consider you overdue if you missed your estimate for any of them. Talking to Center was reserved for the big boys. A vestige of the old FSS flight-following system remains as the lake-reporting and mountain-reporting services available in some areas.

Most pilots assume that in the event of an emergency landing they'll have ample time to get a call off to someone to tell them of their plight. Unfortunately, this isn't always the case. If you're fighting a weather problem you may be forced down gradually by lowering ceilings; by the time you desperately want to let the rest of the world know your location, you're too low to communicate. Even if you have plenty of altitude, it's easy to let time and altitude dwindle away while you troubleshoot the problem or hunt for a field. As an example, I flew a search for an airplane reported to be down in the local area, and it turned out that the pilot actually had bounced to a stop on the ground before he found time to talk to FSS. Fortunately, he was only a few miles from a VOR, so he still had communications at ground level.

What Happens If You Don't Arrive?

If a problem arises and you need someone to start looking for you, don't count on getting off a message at the last minute. The ancient and honorable VFR flight plan can be a lifesaver due to its passive ability to trigger a response, and you'll save a lot of wasted man-hours in speculative search efforts by revealing your plans. If you don't arrive at your filed destination by 30 minutes after your ETA, a communications search will be started. If this is fruitless, an alert notice is sent out on the teletype network to all FSS facilities along your route. If another hour goes by with no word from you, a full-blown search mission will be mounted, coordinated by the Air Force Rescue Coordination Center at Scott AFB in Illinois. The hard work of the actual search is usually delegated to the volunteers of the Civil Air Patrol, with assistance from the military, law-enforcement personnel, and local rescue units. The success of a search mission varies, depending on how closely you kept to your planned route and how cleverly you managed to conceal your downed bird. If your ELT works as advertised, there's a good chance that you won't have to wait until spring to be rescued.

When Should You File?

As an example of a good use of a VFR flight plan, let's use the old vacation scenario. Jack and Judy load up and head west, telling their coworkers they're going to California and Oregon on their vacation. One day into the trip, they meet with disaster and slide to an ignominious halt on a snow-covered hillside, uninjured but miles from anywhere. Now, who's going to look for them? Maybe after a couple of weeks roll by somebody will happen to remember the happy vacationers. "What ever happened to Jack and Judy? Did anyone get a card from them?" If Jack and Judy are incapacitated by injuries, or if the weather is extreme, their bones may not be found until the snow melts. Their ELT will go off and bring the calvary riding to the rescue—if they put batteries in it, or if the antenna didn't tear away. Personally, I would like someone to know my intentions, in addition to carrying the little box in the back.

But file a flight plan on every trip? Obviously, no. I doubt that the FSS network would be able to handle the load. So long as *someone* is expecting you to be *somewhere* at a certain *time*, there's little need for a more official flight plan. If you tell your spouse you'll be heading to Missoula today and stopping by Butte tomorrow, and you make a practice of calling if you're late, that's sort of a flight plan. Or, if you have appointments to keep in Hot Springs this morning, your secretary probably will start getting inquiries if you don't show up. If the airplane is a rented one, there was probably some discussion of your intentions. In all cases, make sure somebody at your home base knows who to contact if you're overdue; the nearest FSS will get things started, if given the word. But whenever you're going to be out of contact with the rest of the world for an extended period of time, file a flight plan.

There will be times when filing is impractical, as when arriving at or departing from a remote boondocks airport lacking even telephones. You may not know what your ability to close the flight plan will be and you may want to stay off the record to prevent a needless search being starting. Or your schedule and route may not be clear at the time of your departure. These are valid reasons to fly without a flight plan, but even so, you can check in over a VOR now and then with a position report, or make a weather check by giving your location and intentions; this will put you on record as being somewhere at a certain time, a fact that can help the searchers immensely.

How to File

Filing a flight plan can be done in person, by phone when checking the weather, or by radio once you're airborne. The latter ties up the airwaves and the FSS air-ground specialist, so it should be avoided as much as possible. Get familiar with the flight plan form so you can rattle off the required items in the proper sequence; this helps the FSS specialist write it down the first time and avoids requests for a repeat. Don't give the specialist long descriptions of what each item is; he or she knows the order of the entries, so only short guide words will be necessary.

In most cases, the FSS will hold your flight plan until you report the takeoff by radio, but if an airborne check-in is not possible (as when flying a no-radio airplane), you can be assumed off at a certain time, with an agreement to call back by phone if you can't get the bird into the air. Once activated, the flight plan goes on the wire to the FSS responsible for your destination airport, and it now becomes their responsibility to call for the bloodhounds if you don't show up. Therefore, if you change your mind or run late, the proper party to inform is not the FSS with which you filed the flight plan, but the destination FSS. If you are forced to stop midway in your flight, any FSS can teletype a cancellation or an extension of an arrival time to the FSS holding your flight plan.

Please make sure you close the flight plan. Don't assume the control tower does it (they don't and won't), and don't tell anyone else to do it for you. Just call your cancellation in by radio or get to a phone promptly after landing. Failure to do so may result in your being awakened from a sound sleep by a posse of very irate rescue personnel who won't take kindly to your being snug in your warm little bed when they are out beating the bushes for you.

Don't forget about your old friend, the VFR flight plan. It's still a good idea, even though an attempt to discontinue it has been made more than once. Use it whenever no one else is going to be looking for you, for your family's sake if not for your own.

Part II
Traffic and Airports

Chapter 8
The Midair Menace

There is a continuing need for us pilots to remind ourselves that other airplanes are up there with us. One of the most commonly cited reasons for flight test failure is a lack of vigilance by the applicant; other airplanes come into view and pass with no recognition because the pilot is deeply engrossed in the cockpit tasks. I'd have to call it a fair bust, even if it were one of my own students, because I might be up there myself someday, and I sure want the pilot to be looking for me.

Statistics

What is a midair collision, typically? Statistics show that about 85 percent of all recorded midairs occur between small general aviation aircraft in clear weather. The chance of a midair occurring while both aircraft are under IFR control in actual instrument conditions is rather remote and, despite all the headlines and movie hoopla, airliners do not run a great risk of being attacked by little airplanes. Large, high-performance airplanes are generally separated from the smaller general aviation fleet by reason of operating desires; the jets need to go high as soon as possible, while we normally want to remain as low as practical.

The 25 to 35 persons killed each year in some 50 midair collisions are a miniscule part of total aircraft accidents, a far less serious problem than weather accidents or poor flying skill during takeoff and landing. Any accident is one too many, of course, and it behooves us to take such steps as are reasonably proper to prevent it. Understanding the circumstances behind most midairs will help alert us to the problem, perhaps motivating us to look around a bit harder.

Where Do Midairs Occur?

The large majority of collisions happen on or within a few miles of an airport. An old railroader once observed of airports, "We have one track out on the main line but several of them coming into the station. You fellows have lots of tracks up there but only one here at your depot. That ain't too smart." Unfortunately, he's right; the common target of all airplanes converging on an airport is the approach end of the duty runway, making it only natural that collision accidents will arise during this phase of operation.

While midairs do occasionally occur within controlled airport traffic patterns, the bulk of them happen at small, non-controlled fields, where discipline often slips and pilots tend to do their own thing. VFR daylight weather usually prevails, although we would imagine that haze contributes to many of the midairs. California has always led the country in midairs, logically enough, since it has a high aircraft population in areas noted for low-visibility conditions.

Often the two tangled airplanes were maneuvering for takeoff or landing when they got together; one may have been taking off while the other was in a nose-high approach to landing, or both airplanes may have been on final approach at the same time. I once experienced a near-miss at a non-controlled FSS-only field, reporting on a two-mile straight-in final only to hear another airplane call a two-mile final a few seconds later. He and I compared notes hurriedly, and found that he was above my left wing while I was below the right side of his instrument panel, converging nicely. That was my last straight-in approach at an uncontrolled field.

Dual instruction plays a major role in midair collisions, as both occupants of the airplane are busy teaching and learning with minimal time left over for looking outside. Flight instructors hold the key to instilling vigilance in future pilots, however; if the CFI makes a point of looking outside himself, locking the control wheel in neutral until the student has cleared his turning airspace, and otherwise emphasizing the seriousness of the matter, an instinct to look will be fostered in the student. On the other hand, if he sits there with paralysis of the neck and eyeballs, so will his students.

How to Avoid Midairs

One of the best ways of avoiding near-misses with high-speed IFR traffic is to fly where they aren't. Learn which runway is active when passing near a busy field, and which approach is in use, by listening to ATIS or the tower chatter. Monitor the approach control frequency in your area even if not in contact yourself. With an idea of where the inbound traffic is coming from, you can steer clear of the "dump areas" of descending jets. Just make sure your deviations around the big airport don't take you unknowingly through a small airport's traffic pattern at low altitude.

The perfect-visibility aircraft does not exist; therefore, we must recognize that our airplanes have blind spots and clear them for traffic constantly, particularly in the vicinity of an airport. Adjust your seat for best vision, if it cranks up and down; too high and you may not be able to see out the side windows without ducking, too low and you will have a large area obscured by the panel. Raise a wingtip to check for descending traffic in your high-wing airplane; dip a wing or turn slightly to look underneath your low-wing bird. Lean across and look out the right side of your airplane if you don't have an eagle-eyed passenger sitting over there to help you. If you see a shadow on the ground that isn't yours, find out where the bogey is—*fast*.

Remember that converging airplanes do not move in relation to each other; this makes it doubly hard to spot a midair threat. First, moving targets are picked up much easier than stationary ones by our scanning glance and, second, if the target is in a blind spot (such as windshield posts), it tends to stay there. A clean windshield naturally makes such motionless targets easier to detect, but don't forget the side windows also. Strobes and high-visibility paint colors will help, if you're in a position to determine the airplane's outfitting. However, even the most dull-finished airplane can be seen before it hits you, if you're looking.

Looking Around

Not looking at all is the biggest midair hazard. As a CFI, I ride with a great many pilots and habitually evaluate them; very few of my flight review applicants, for instance, exhibit adequate vigilance for other aircraft. Looking must be methodical; clear the airspace you are about to occupy before you go there. If making a left turn, don't just glance out the left window; look back over your left shoulder as well for that airplane in front of which you're liable to be turning.

When making a landing approach, don't stare at the runway while on base leg; look up final approach once in a while. Don't just take the runway after completing your runup, with a quick glance at the downwind leg; look on the final approach and base legs as well, even it takes a full circle to do so. It only takes one unsettling experience, such as having an airplane zoom down right in front of you just after you've opened the throttle for takeoff, to convince you to look around more. But you may never live through all the bad experiences to complete your learning!

Don't be tempted into making right-hand or straight-in approaches just because you think nobody is around; the few seconds saved aren't worth the risk. Enter patterns at the proper altitude, usually 800 feet AGL, so all other airplanes will be visible out of your windows instead of hiding above and below a wing or windowline.

Use the radio for position advisories, but do not rely on such calls exclusively; there are no-radio aircraft out there, and there is always the klutz who is still on Center frequency when he hits the pattern. Look outside even while you're announcing your intentions over the wireless.

We can seek all possible help from ATC radar for traffic advisories, and we can equip our airplanes to the hilt with lights and radios, but the simple fact of avoiding most midair collisions is the need to use our eyeballs. There are more and more airplanes out there every year, so don't get complacent just because you don't see them. It only takes one to ruin your day!

Chapter 9

The Uncontrolled Airport

"Hey, look, here he comes again!" called the acting ramp scout at the small country airport. His function was to alert us to any inbound aircraft while we occupied chairs in the deep shade, sparing us from sunburn and sore feet. The subject in question had already made several passes at what seemed to be a perfectly ample amount of runway, wisely adding power for the waveoff when he turned out to be higher than a tobacco barn at midfield.

After the first go-around we had made book on the number of attempts he would require, and so far the holder of the lucky number four had resigned himself to enriching the eventual winner. As the object of our wagers came out of his base-leg turn, however, another factor entered the equation in the form of a light twin on a long straight-in final approach. "They're going to get close," opined the ramp watcher, and we rose from our chairs to assume a sprinting position.

The twin gave no sign of noticing the aircraft on a close-in base leg, and the other pilot had all of his attention fixed on the runway of his heart's desire. He reached the final approach course slightly ahead of the twin, and as he banked onto final the twin's pilot saw the flash of movement and pulled up. Another midair was averted—one less headline to provide grist for the FAA's plans to expand positive control.

The hapless go-around veteran made an uneventful full-stop landing this time, but as he turned around on the runway to taxi back to the hangars he encountered—who else—the light twin on short final. Following his waveoff, the pilot of the twin had made a tight 360° turn on final at an altitude of 300 feet AGL, maximum, and did not count on the preceding aircraft still being a factor. The taxiing pilot headed for the grass just as the twin started his second go-

35

around—more wasted gasoline, more heated tempers. The crowd returned to the chairs, ready to break up the fight when the twin's pilot caught up with the other aviator.

"Didn't think I'd ever get down," said the lone occupant of the first airplane as he disembarked in full view of our group. "Could I getcha to sign my logbook? I'm running a little behind on my solo cross-country with all these go-arounds." One of the locals moved quickly to oblige, anxious to finish the act before the twin pilot shut down.

"Hey, don't anybody listen to the radio around here?" bellowed the many-motor's driver as he climbed out onto his wingwalk. "I called three times and nobody answered me." He cast a withering look in the direction of the student and headed for the lounge, leaving his airplane in a position that blockaded two hangars, the student's airplane, and part of a taxiway. It was time for action and education.

"Come on, boys, let's get this kid out of here," I said. "Get on that wing and help me push this heavy iron back a few feet." I squinted toward the office, hoping the twin pilot was watching. Fortunately he left his brake off, so I did not have to soil his carpet with my dirty boots. I gave a few words of encouragement to the student about working on his approaches, and pointed him back toward the big city airport from whence he had come. Then I walked over to the lounge to look up the twin's pilot.

He had cooled off only a few degrees, still mouthing about the silence on Unicom and lame-brained country cowboys who wouldn't get off the runway. "What frequency were you on?" I asked. "Unicom, 122.8" he said. "Isn't that what they use here?"

"Nope," sez I. "The Sectional I used to find this place had no frequency shown at all, so 122.9 is the advisory channel for safety messages, according to the *Airman's Information Manual*."

"Guess I should have reported my straight-in approach on that channel," he said. What he *didn't* say was that he probably hadn't unfolded a Sectional in some years, preferring enroute charts and Jepp books for his navigation.

I bored in. "No, what you *should* have done was fly at least part of a traffic pattern. A straight-in approach is a great way to meet people . . . in midair." We sparred a few more rounds, finally agreeing that you certainly have to be careful around these small airports, and parted more or less friends.

Expect the Unexpected

With the increase in the aircraft population and a decrease in the

Fig. 9-1. Located near a residential area, this convenient small airport has Unicom and two runways, one turf and one paved. The lack of taxiways means one should give way to landing aircraft when departing.

number of public-use airports, we can expect more and more scenarios like the foregoing. The training texts furnish 25-year-old illustrations, of 45° traffic-pattern entry paths, segmented circles, and wind Ts, but today that's only half the story. Pilots must be prepared to cope with the non-textbook happenings that can arise every day at uncontrolled airports.

If there happen to be a couple of other airplanes in the pattern, who goes first? If a go-around becomes necessary, how is re-sequencing accomplished? How close does one operate to another airplane?

These are real-life questions at non-tower airports. Nobody is up there in a glass cage playing referee. That leaves the pilots to make all the decisions. Unicom is just an advisory channel, an electronic wind sock, nothing more. The first rule to remember when operating at an uncontrolled field is to take nothing for granted. Be expecting that other pilot to do something stupid, and keep an eye on him every second.

Do not assume your traffic advisory calls were heard. There are still plenty of airplanes out there without radios, or if they have one the volume may be turned down or it may be on the wrong frequency. Nevertheless, it's wise to make a call to Unicom or "Podunk Traffic" before entering the pattern as well as before taking the runway for departure. The suggested calls on each leg of the pattern, clearing the runway, prior to taxi, etc., are even better, if you have time.

What Is a Traffic Pattern?

A traffic pattern is a rectangular box around the airport, a path airplanes should follow to maintain an orderly flow of traffic. This simple definition gets ignored by many pilots, unfortunately. The FARs have very little to say about traffic patterns, mentioning only that all turns shall be made to the left unless otherwise specified and that right-of-way belongs to the airplane at the lowest altitude. By convention, entries to the downwind leg, that part of the pattern flown beside the runway opposite to the direction of landing, should be made at midfield on a 45° angle, making it easier to avoid departing aircraft and to merge with traffic remaining in the pattern. Height of the traffic pattern varies with location, but in noncongested areas it is most commonly 800 feet AGL. It does help immensely if all aircraft enter at the same altitude, so high and low-wing airplanes can see each other.

If you don't know the wind direction, take a look at the wind sock before committing yourself to land. If the sock is limp, winds are calm, so keep an eye on the opposite end of the runway for opposing traffic, or on other runways if there are more than one.

By regulation, right-hand approaches at fields with a left-hand pattern are *verboten*. It is senseless to be out of step with everyone else, but every so often we see someone try it, usually attempting to save a few minutes of rental time. You may think you are the only airplane out there, but remember what we said in the previous section: It's the one you *don't* see that gets you. A straight-in approach, on the other hand, is quasilegal, but it's dumb, because an airplane on a long final can be nearly invisible to other traffic.

It may occasionally be convenient to make a base-leg entry to an uncontrolled pattern, to avoid a 180° turn on the downwind leg, but such an entry does assure at least one turn before turning final, giving a measure of visibility. Never, however, make a base-leg entry if there is traffic on downwind. In addition, my old daddy taught me to look both ways before crossing a street, so I always look out the right window before turning final, in case's someone's out there dragging in it.

Runway manners are every bit as important at an uncontrolled field as at a controlled airport. You should plan on clearing the runway promptly after touchdown, so land and roll out to take advantage of any exits that were noted before landing. In the absence of a taxiway, most pilots will taxi back on the runway rather than risk an unknown sod surface, so leave time for the preceding aircraft to taxi clear. If you are talking to another airplane and want to make arrangements with that pilot about landing short or rolling out long, fine and dandy, but in the absence of such a scheme, follow another plane with your hand on the throttle, ready to go around.

If forced to make a waveoff, climb out beside the runway so you can see other aircraft and ascend back to the downwind leg. Don't try a tight, low, 360° turn back onto final; the residents won't like it, the other pilots may not see you, and if the engine quits you'll be in a hazardous position. On the other hand, don't fly a superextended pattern just because there's another airplane ahead of you. Use only enough airspace to give breathing room. Generally speaking, a half-mile is close enough when following another airplane, and that assumes you can match speeds. A proper traffic pattern size gives a final approach of one-half to one mile in length; a two-mile final is a bit wasteful of fuel unless it is required due to a string of airplanes landing ahead of you. It also leaves too much open space, tempting other aircraft to unknowingly turn inside you on a closer base leg.

Using the Radio

The proper advisory frequency is the charted Unicom channel, usually 122.7, 122.8 or 123.0, used for position reports even if no one answers. However, if there is an active FSS on the field, 123.6 is the channel designated for airport advisories. During hours when the FSS is closed, 123.6 remains as the advisory frequency, utilized for blind traffic calls. If there is no published frequency, 122.9 is the final option. Always start your call with the airport name: "Podunk traffic, this is Cessna one-four-two-five Victor, turning downwind for one-two." In this manner, inhabitants of other traffic patterns won't have to listen to your entire call to learn your location. Calls on base leg, final approach, taxiing back, and clearing the runway should be made only if you don't walk on someone else's transmission.

When parking, try not to block other aircraft, taxiways, or the fuel pump area. Unless there are acres of ramp space, always ask someone where to park before you leave for town, even if you think you have chosen a vacant spot.

Life at small country airports doesn't have to be traumatic, but unfamiliar pilots must remember that they are strangers in a strange land, and they must keep an eye out for the unexpected. Take a little more time than you might when flying in a controlled airport environment, making sure you are conforming to the flow of traffic and aren't getting in anyone's way. Even the busiest uncontrolled fields can be safely negotiated if you just don't insist on having everything your own way.

Chapter 10

The Grass Strip

Creating an airport can be about as simple as measuring out a plot of vacant pastureland and informing the FAA that you would like the meadow listed as an approved landing facility. *Approved* means little more than that the field was once usable in some fashion and that it posed no hazard to existing airports. Thus it comes as no surprise that of the 15,000 U.S. airports, only about one third have paved runways.

For those of us who grew up, aeronautically speaking, with pavement under our tires, landing on grass can be a refreshing change—or perhaps a bit of a shock if the field is poorly maintained. Grass fields can vary widely in their suitability for aircraft use, and the same runway can change radically with advancing seasons. Before you flight plan into a strip known only as a magenta circle on the chart, take time to review some grass field facts.

What Are Little Grass Fields Made Of?

First, that beckoning runway may not be grass at all; the open circle symbol means only that the strip is unpaved (or has pavement less than 1500 feet in length). The surface could be carefully-groomed bluegrass, native prairie sod, cinders, packed sand, or just plain dirt. Unless you have reliable information of a recent nature, treat an unfamiliar turf airfield as possibly unsafe, and have a paved alternate within range should it prove to be unusable when you arrive. Even such an unknown factor as a three-inch rainfall the night before could prove to be your undoing, should you touch down on the soggy surface.

Naturally, the type of aircraft used will influence your decision about a turf field. Taildraggers generally have a larger measure of utility on such strips, since they tend to have lower touchdown speeds and less landing gear resistance on takeoff. Light twins, on the other hand, should be used only on the best-maintained grass runways. The ideal turf runway is well-drained to dry out quickly after a shower, evenly graded to avoid humps and hollows, and covered with a dense, cultivated sod. If the grass is kept down to two inches in height and rolled frequently to compact the soil, no finer experience exists than sinking into the carpet with scarcely a sound from the tires. It beats the "chirp" of expended rubber any time.

How to Use the Grass Runway

Allow 50 percent more distance for your aircraft's operation from a grass runway in average condition; if the vegetation is over the tops of the tires, double or triple the takeoff distance shown in the handbook. Landing is generally less troublesome, as the drag of the grass works to your favor, but brakes can be rendered inoperative by tall grass wrapping around the wheels, and wet grass can be as slick as icy pavement. Stopping is also made more difficult by the aircraft's vigorous bouncing on rough sod, since the wheels are only in momentary skidding contact with the surface.

Successful operation from a sod field will depend on your familiarity with rough-field procedure. Most turf strips are anything but smooth, so land with the last ounce of airspeed used up, remaining aloft as long as possible before subjecting the landing gear to the punishment of the rough surface. The nosegear should be held off until elevator control is lost and the stick kept full back even after the nose comes down. Use brakes only as needed, to keep excess weight off the nosegear.

Takeoffs should be made by transferring the aircraft's weight to the wings as soon as possible, relieving the landing gear of stress before the speed builds up. If flaps are available to increase lift, use the recommended maximum setting. If the nosewheel is not lifted out of the grass early in the run, normal takeoff speed might be impossible to achieve within the limits of the runway. So full aft stick should be used to bring the nosewheel off, then back pressure used as needed to maintain the nose-up attitude. As soon as the aircraft begins to feel light, a slight amount of additional back pressure on the stick will bring liftoff. Follow with an immediate level-off into a shallow climb, gaining speed before leaving ground effect.

Two seasons of the year call for extra caution around turf fields—early spring and early summer. During the last weeks of winter, daytime thawing and nighttime freezes keep moisture near the soil's surface, making the runway unusable except while frozen in the morning hours. Early summer brings the hay season, when many private farm strips are allowed to grow up knee-high so the owners can harvest the hay and seed crop.

Is the Field Okay for Use?

So much for the art of handling the airplane on grass, but how do you judge the field's condition before use? Walk the entire strip if at all possible, checking for new gopher holes, muddy spots, and rocks. The limits of a grass runway should be marked in some manner to keep pilots away from ditches and other hazards. Permanent markings can be half-buried tires, reflectors, or wooden markers on posts. Temporary flags on short stakes can also be helpful. Nothing should be used that would be a hazard to the airplane if struck accidentally.

If the surface proves reasonably solid and free of obstructions, and you decide to give it a try, taxi at reduced speed to lessen the shock to the landing gear and airframe. If you inadvertently bog down in a muddy spot, use full aft stick and lots of power to keep moving, so the tires will remain afloat long enough to reach solid ground. Once stopped, the tires sink deeper and deeper until escape is impossible. Small nosewheels, when allowed to sink into the mud,

Fig. 10-1. Because grass strips look like the rest of the countryside, one must be certain to land in the designated area, and not off the runway itself. Here we are about to land on a 50-foot wide grass runway between rows of field crops, an easy decision.

43

give the propeller a downward thrust line that turns the airplane into a mole; I have seen nosegear fairings burrowed completely out of sight.

If you are aloft, the runway's condition is naturally more difficult to ascertain. Circle overhead at pattern altitude to look for bare touchdown and rollout tracks, a clue to the best area to use. Note wet areas, marked by darker colored soil and grass. If a breeze is blowing, watch for ripples in the grass like waves on a lake; grass tall enough to ripple is too tall for landing upon.

When the grass is worn or nonexistent, look for ruts in the dirt, so you can avoid those bone-jarrers as you touch down. Washouts will show up from the pattern, as will terraces and waterways. After the high recon, make a low pass down the runway at 50 to 100 feet to drag the field, keeping well above stall speed but slower than cruise. Look for the smaller holes unseen from higher altitude, and watch for standing water shining beneath the grass cover. Then apply full power and climb back to normal pattern height for your approach, if all looks well.

Making Contact

Due to their unimproved nature, grass fields seem to have more than their share of obstructions on the approach lane, as well as vagaries in their terrain. The obstructions are best handled by a steep, full-flap approach (flaps are needed for the soft-field touchdown anyway). Sloping terrain is another matter, affecting both approach and touchdown.

If the runway slopes uphill, the approach will look high when it really isn't, and you may wind up needing a last-minute shot of throttle to clear the fence. More-than-normal back pressure is needed to flare into the nose-up attitude demanded by the runway's slope, and the effective sink rate may be great enough to require power during the flare, but at least the rollout will be short with gravity's assistance.

Landing downhill means going around if touchdown is not made in the first couple hundred feet of runway. The approach will be partially to blame, since the slope of the ground makes you look about right when you're actually going to land long. Practice those spot landings for such an occurrence, so you can get the tires planted as soon as possible, and don't be ashamed to open the throttle once again if the ground just keeps falling away from you during your attempt to land.

The rolling, undulating strip can be a problem for the unwary, especially if you neglect to hold the stick full aft as you contact a rise in the ground. It is best to touch down in the low spot just before ascending a rise, so you can decelerate on the way up and stay solidly on the ground as you go over the hump at the top. Pilots taking off from rolling strips should plan to lift off on the downslope, perhaps with an over-the-hill start to ensure lifting off before passing the low spot and encountering rising ground.

Finding a sod strip from the air may take some doing in itself, as grass fields look like . . . well, grass fields. The charted location will provide a place to start, answering such questions as which side of the railroad tracks, how far from town, or between which two roads the strip lies. Once you are sure of the general area, start looking for the long, open space required for a runway and the inevitable wind sock. In the absence of boundary markers, ascertain the center of the runway with care; look for a worn track and for obvious indications of mowing.

Taking Care of the Airplane

Preparing the airplane for sod strip operation should include service to the shock struts; a flat strut is only a minor annoyance on paved runways, but a severe threat to the airframe structure on rough fields. Keeping the tires slightly underinflated can improve shock-absorbing ability and increase footprint area. It might be wise to remove wheel fairings, especially during wet weather, so they can't fill up with mud and frozen slush. Check the carburetor air filter every time you're outside the airplane; it will require frequent cleaning to remove grass seeds and clippings.

Summing up, landing on a good grass airport is a sensuous experience worth all the extra precautions. Even Learjets have been successfully operated from grass, so if the field is long and smooth enough, have no qualms about using it. Some of those unpaved strips are right where you've been wanting to go, and with a little respect and judgment you can probably use most of them.

Chapter 11

The Tower-Controlled Airport

Not everyone is fortunate enough to be able to learn to fly at a tower-controlled airport. After all, there are only a few hundred towers among the 15,000 U.S. airports. Thus, a lot of pilots gain only a nodding acquaintance with tower procedures.

In many cases, the newly rated pilot remains deathly afraid of doing the wrong thing at a controlled field and bringing down the full wrath of the Federal Aviation Administration as a result of his ineptitude. Therefore, he avoids busy airports like the plague, which only makes matters worse, since lack of use quickly dulls the meager skills he had acquired when fulfilling the licensing requirements. Confidence in any piloting operation comes from knowing in advance what is likely to happen and how you are going to make it happen.

There is, of course, no need to fear the controlled airport. The tower operators aren't out to write tickets; all they want to do is to keep the airplanes moving safely. Filing a violation is done only as a last resort, when a pilot displays an utter disregard for cooperation and willfully creates a hazard to others. Tower personnel don't like the paperwork of violations and as long as the pilot is honest with them, minor miscues can be overlooked. So much for the fear of towers.

In some respects, using a field with a control tower is actually simpler than flying into a non-controlled airport. The tower controller assigns runway and landing sequence for you, and you will probably be allowed to approach directly from your present position, be it straight-in, right-hand base leg, or whatever, rather than be locked into the standard pattern of a non-tower airport. All you need do is acknowledge receipt of tower instructions and carry them out, and the more familiar you are with procedures, the easier this becomes.

Arrival Procedures

Let's say you are headed for Smogville International, a little jittery about this first trip into the city for several months. Studying the chart while enroute, you note the pattern of the runway layout, and look for the letters ATIS with a frequency under the airport name. If the airport has such an Automatic Terminal Information Service, listening on that frequency before announcing your arrival will help immensely. ATIS gives a recorded playback of weather and wind data, runway in use, and any NOTAMS critical to operation on the field. A code word lets the tower operator know you have listened to ATIS if you say "have information Kilo" or whatever the current password is.

If there is no ATIS, listen for a few moments to the conversations on the primary tower frequency (the one shown on the chart after elevation and runway length) and you will be able to glean essentially the same information as ATIS. Then you can tell the tower "I have the numbers," to let them know to save their breath. Without some tipoff, the tower folks are honor-bound to give each new arrival full weather and traffic info; using ATIS or listening first makes a friend right off the bat.

Having listened to get the picture, look over your situation, in light of the runway in use, to anticipate what the tower will want you to do. If runway 17 is in use, and you are approaching from directly east of the field, it would be logical to expect a clearance to enter left traffic for 17, either a downwind entry or a base-leg entry. If coming in from north of the field, you might anticipate a request to report on a long final, straight in for 17. Mentally prepared, you are much more likely to understand a controller's rapid-fire delivery, as well as being on top of any misunderstanding.

In some cases, your first contact may be with Approach Control, rather than the local tower controller, particularly at airports with an ARSA (airport radar service area), an extra layer of airspace up to 4000 feet AGL and 10 miles in radius. This only involves using one more frequency and picking up your clearance somewhat farther out from the airport; otherwise everything is the same. If Approach Control's assistance is desired, ATIS may give the frequency, or the control tower may suggest that you go over to Approach on frequency such-and-such when you call in too far out. In a pinch, Flight Service will gladly provide it for you; Approach Control frequencies may be shown on the border of the chart, and are published in the *Airman's Information Manual*. However, unless the airport has a Terminal Control Area (TCA) or an ARSA, contact with Approach Control is optional.

Remember, a basic control tower only has jurisdiction over the Airport Traffic Area, defined as a five-mile radius of the airport up to 3000 feet above the surface. Cooperation on the pilot's part includes not running right up to the traffic area boundary before hollering "I want in." An advance call gives time for several blocked-out transmissions and pauses for a lull in traffic before actually violating the traffic area. Make your first report at some prominent point well outside the five-mile limit so the controller will instantly know where you are. However, something like "seven miles east" will suffice if you don't see anything clearly marked on the chart. Be sure to listen briefly with the volume up before pushing the mike button, so as not to interrupt another transmission.

When making the initial call-up, keep it simple but complete. Tell 'em who you are, where you are, and what you want to do: "Smogville Tower, this is Cessna one-two-three-six-Quebec, over the stadium, landing, with Kilo, over." You've said it all, the tower controller has only to decide what to do with you. The reply probably will assign a closer-in reporting point and an entry path to follow: "Cessna three-six-Quebec, report on left base to runway one-seven." Since you are not yet in sight, your sequence behind other aircraft cannot be assigned until you report on left base.

Acknowledge all instructions as received and understood by giving your call sign, abbreviated to the last three figures if the tower got it right on the initial call-up. Do not acknowledge unless you did understand; if you aren't sure what he said or what he meant, *now* is the time to say so, not when you're in the middle of a muddle of airplanes. Controllers will talk at a pace acceptable to the pilots they are used to working with and you may not copy everything the first time; tell 'em "Say again, please" until you do understand, then give them the "three-six-Quebec" acknowledgment.

After the first call-up you have only to fly closer to the airport, following the approach path requested by the tower. Be watching for other traffic as you hear them contact the tower, so you have them located before the tower gives them to you as traffic.

Reporting your arrival at the assigned point is a simple pronouncement: "Cessna three-six-Quebec, left base for one-seven." The controller now has you in sight and identified, and issues either a "cleared to land" or a sequence, such as "number two, behind the red Bonanza on one-mile final." Acknowledge all tower instructions, and if given sequence behind another aircraft, let the tower know whether or not you see him. Say either "I've got the traffic" or "no contact." If you acknowledge having your traffic in sight, separation becomes largely your responsibility. If you report no contact, the controller will point out the other aircraft in greater detail, or will steer you well clear.

When following another aircraft, do not crowd in closer than 3000 feet, or you may be asked to go around. On the other hand, don't waste everybody's time by using a two-mile interval. Use your head by keeping your speed up when following a fast airplane until just before landing. If you know your traffic is going to be slow, plan on letting it all hang out (lowering flaps) to maintain your position, or S-turn slightly. If you are number one and you know you have traffic behind you, be a good neighbor and keep the pattern in close and reasonably fast.

You will normally be "cleared to land" only after the airplane ahead has turned off the runway, but as long as you have been assigned a sequence, continue your approach, expecting the clearance before you touch down. Should the tower remain silent, an inquiry might be in order: "Is three-six-Quebec cleared to land?" But if the controller is talking three-miles-a-minute to another aircraft, go ahead and land as long as there is no conflict in view. Technically, you are in violation, but as long as a normal traffic flow is maintained, everybody's happy.

If you do feel a go-around is necessary, get the airplane organized first, then advise the tower as quickly as possible what you are doing: "Three-six-Quebec is going around, we'll try another landing." The tower may tell you "make left traffic, report downwind," or if the pattern is clearly defined, may just say to follow the aircraft ahead. Reporting on downwind is tantamount to asking for a landing clearance, so if you want to do anything different than the previous circuits, this is the time to advise the tower: "Three-six-Quebec downwind, this will be a full stop" advises the controller that you are finished touching and going, for instance. "What are your intentions?" is his request for information.

Getting Around on the Ground

After touchdown, head for a convenient exit as soon as you have good ground-handling control; don't come to a full crawl first and cause a go-around. The runway is hot property, so don't keep it any longer than is necessary. Stay on the tower frequency until turning off, then check in on the Ground Control channel unless advised not to by the tower. It is not necessary to stop while calling up Ground Control; as long as no conflicting traffic is coming at you, it's acceptable to let the airplane roll during the few seconds before contact.

Hold your position if another airplane is approaching, of course. If you don't know Ground Control's frequency, fear not; the tower will probably tell you "Contact Ground Control on point six when clear," or you can ask them. There are basically four frequencies in general use—121.6, 121.7, 121.8 and 121.9, of which point-nine is the most prevalent—but some newer towers have odd Ground Control channels.

If you know where you are going, tell Ground Control what you're doing when you check in: "Three-six-Quebec, just clear of one-seven, going to Gulf Air". If you don't know where you're going, say so, asking for transient services or the terminal. The controller can then take you by the hand, leading you through the maze of taxiways to the ramp. Tower personnel cannot recommend parking or service facilities for you, so watch for flag persons or serve yourself as you see fit.

Getting Out Again

After finishing your business, departure is equally simple. Listen first to ATIS for any changes since you arrived, then advise Ground Control of your location and desires: "Smogville ground, Cessna one-two-three-six-Quebec, at Gulf Air with Lima, taxi for takeoff, over." Turn on a rotating beacon or pull forward a few feet to help the controller pick you out of a line of airplanes. "Three-six-Quebec, taxi to runway one-seven via north on Alpha" may be the reply. Taxiways are commonly named by letters of the phonetic alphabet, so acknowledge, then look for a sign with the letter A on it. Yellow center strips mean taxiways, as do blue edge lights; don't trundle out onto a wide taxiway with white markings and clear lights, because that's a runway!

You are cleared to cross intersecting runways as long as Ground Control said "Cleared *to* runway one-seven." If the clearance was simply "Three-six-Quebec, runway one-seven, hold short of two-four," be alert for an intersecting runway somewhere enroute to one-seven, and stop short of it if you haven't been cleared to cross by that time.

In some cases your initial call-up will be to a clearance-delivery frequency rather than ground control, as advised by the ATIS. This extra step is part of the procedure to use at a Terminal Radar Service Area (TRSA) or ARSA, wherein the approach controller will assist in your departure from the area. The clearance delivery person will assign you a heading to fly after takeoff, a transponder code, and a frequency on which to contact Departure Control after takeoff. As with the use of Approach Control during the arrival, the procedure is optional at a TRSA and may be declined by telling ground control "Negative Stage-three service" when you request taxi instructions. However, if you are only an occasional visitor to the airport, it is wise to use radar for both arrival and departure.

When arriving at the runway, a double yellow line perpendicular to the taxiway marks the "hold-short" line, which you are not to cross without tower permission. Do your runup off to one side of the taxiway so other pilots may pass you to depart if they're ready first. You may, of course, use an intersection short of the runway's end as the start of your takeoff roll, so long as you advise Ground Control of your intentions first, but remember, the responsibility is *yours* if it turns out you needed more.

Following the runup, switch to tower frequency and advise "Cessna three-six-Quebec, ready for takeoff on one-seven" (or "midfield one-seven" if making an intersection departure). It is common procedure to advise the tower of your direction of flight unless you are using Stage III service, such as "straight out to Blytheville," and the tower may solicit this information.

You may receive an immediate "Cleared for takeoff," you may be advised to "Hold short," or you can be told to "Pull into position and hold." The latter means to get out onto the runway and line up, but to wait for a "Cleared for takeoff" while traffic gets off the runway. If the tower says "Make an immediate takeoff or hold short," it means haste is needed because of landing traffic, so if you elect to go, get moving first and acknowledge on the roll. After you break ground the tower will advise you when to switch to Departure Control, if you are in a TRSA, ARSA, or a TCA. In any case, monitor the last assigned frequency until clear of the airport traffic area.

Remember, control towers are provided as a service to the pilot, so don't be afraid to venture near the busy patterns. Use these fields, and soon you will find that picking up the mike and asking for a clearance is as simple as talking to Unicom. Practice makes it easy.

Chapter 12

Guidelines for TCAs

"Hoo-boy, I'm not going anywhere near *that* place; they've got a TCA over there!" This fearful attitude keeps many perfectly capable pilots from using an airport surrounded by a Terminal Control Area, all because they feel inadequate to cope with the procedures involved. Actually, entering a TCA airport is not very different from going into any busy field; some optional procedures simply become requirements at a TCA.

Take, for example, the equipment requirements. The airplane needs a two-way radio with the appropriate frequencies (usually a 360-channel rig will do), a separate VOR receiver, and a transponder. If entering a Group One TCA, the airplane must also have altitude-reporting capability through the transponder.

What's a TCA, Anyway?

Think of a Terminal Control Area as a giant airport traffic area, which is really all it amounts to. There's no difference in pilot procedure between an airport with Approach Control Terminal Radar Service Area and one with a TCA. In fact, with TRSA coverage you must keep a sharp watch for non-participating traffic when receiving radar advisories, a hazard lacking in most TCA airspace. So you can prepare yourself for the TCA by requesting and utilizing Stage III radar service at some less-congested fields. In this way, you can learn to interpret the radio communications dealing with traffic advisories, vectors, and clearance assignments.

Remember, at a TCA or TRSA airport, more radio frequencies will be used. Look them up and jot them down in the order of use before taking off, and leave room to note clearance details and additional frequencies assigned in flight. The ATIS, or Automatic Terminal Information Service, will be the first channel used, enabling

Fig. 12-1. Larger airports, similar to this one, are designated as Terminal Control Areas and require extra equipment and procedures from pilots. They are, however, no more difficult to enter and exit than any busy tower-controlled field, and should not be written off as "untouchable."

you to pick up the recorded weather, traffic, and NOTAM information. You can listen to the ATIS as many times as you like, but don't do what many pilots do and listen only long enough to pick up the code word without checking the rest of the tape for traffic information and special notices. You might miss something important, such as a taxiway closure or a frequency that is changed, so catch the full broadcast.

From ATIS you can anticipate your arrival path, and also which of the instrument approaches is being used—important information even to VFR pilots, as the type of approach (VOR, ILS, visual) can tip you off as to the arrival procedure being used by jets and heavy aircraft. Check your altimeter setting to make sure your cockpit indication will be the same as your encoded readout on the radar scope, and note the crosswind component you will encounter during landing. Then verify that you will be using the appropriate Approach Control frequency for the initial contact.

Most busy airports have sectorized Approach Control, with separate frequencies for various arrival quadrants, and possibly different channels for VFR versus IFR arrivals. Never fear; if you should call on the wrong frequency, you'll be told to switch to one-two-one-point-five-five or whatever. Always listen for a few

53

seconds before pushing the button to make sure you aren't breaking into a conversation, and have your spiel ready for delivery so you won't have to compose it while holding down the mike button.

What to Say

Every ATC controller is interested in three things: *who* you are, *where* you are, and *what* you want to do. Try to get these three items across in as little time as possible and you'll be cutting down on frequency congestion. Pick out a prominent reporting point for your contact, such as "over Perryville reservoir," "over the stadium," or "over the VOR" (name the station if there is more than one). Look for pennants with underlined place names on your terminal-area (not sectional) chart; these indicate VFR reporting points. A charted VOR airway intersection is known to ATC, of course, and also makes a good reporting point. Begin trying to contact the Approach Controller a few miles outside the TCA, giving yourself time to be acquired as "radar contact" *and* to receive a clearance before you hit the TCA perimeter and become illegal.

Your first call will be something like this: "Downtown Approach, this is Cessna one-two-three-six-Quebec over Backwater with Oscar, landing Downtown, over." In one short sentence you have told the approach controller most of what he needs to know; his response can be "Cessna one-two-three-six-Quebec, squawk one-six-two-seven," the latter being the discrete transponder code which is next in line in the stack for assignment. With the assignment of a code, you are tagged as a specific airplane, complete with N-number and altitude. Acknowledge the transmission with your abbreviated call sign and read back the code as you dial it into the transponder. The next transmission you hope to hear will be "Cessna three-six-Quebec, radar contact 12 miles northwest of the airport, cleared to enter the TCA." This signifies the controller's ability to provide the necessary separation and sequencing for TCA entry. Without hearing these words you are *not* to enter the TCA!

Even if you are equipped with an encoding altimeter, the approach controller will ask you to "Verify 3600," just to make sure you're in agreement with the computer's readout. Approach may also have a groundspeed tagged to your target to help them sequence various types of aircraft.

If asked to "Squawk ident," your reply should be made through the transponder by simply pushing the ident button; no radio reply is needed as you are acknowledging receipt of the instruction by painting as an "ident" return on the radar display. If a second request to ident is made, you can tell the controller you've already idented, in which case you may have a malfunctioning transponder that isn't showing up on the display. At a Group One TCA it is possible to negotiate an entry without an altitude encoder if you have suffered a failure enroute, but a transponder is usually necessary unless prior arrangements have been made.

Being Led by the Hand

After radar contact is established, Approach Control will assign a heading and altitude, or radar vector as it is called, to sequence you with other TCA traffic. The transmission may be "Cessna three-six-Quebec, turn right, heading one-four-zero, maintain three thousand." It is well to read back the instructions unless the controller is already turning his or her attentions elsewhere, but keep it brief, such as "Three-six-Quebec, right to one-four-zero, descending to three thousand." In this way, any misunderstandings will be corrected before you wander too far afield. I might add that it is wise to check your directional gyro for precession before receiving radar vectors; the controller will have enough trouble allowing for a crosswind on your track without tossing in ten degrees or more of precession error between the DG and the magnetic compass.

Jot down the frequency being used when time permits. This gives you a record of the last controller's channel in case you have need to recontact him later. While the control tower will probably be the next voice you'll hear, handoffs are sometimes made if you cross the division line between approach sectors. Whenever you're told to contact a new controller, read back the change by saying "Three-six-Quebec, one-two-four-point-seven" with a brief pause afterward to see if the controller makes any comment. Dial it up promptly, rather than jotting it down first, and listen for traffic a second or two before reporting into the new controller. Your contact will be simply "Downtown Approach, Cessna three-six-Quebec, three thousand," and the reply will be "Roger, three-six-Quebec" unless the new controller has further instructions. If no response is heard after a couple of tries, go back to the previous frequency you had noted earlier and tell that controller you're unable to contact the other controller. If contact is made, write down the new frequency.

Traffic advisories will be issued as needed, whenever a conflict is apparent. If the controller says "Three-six-Quebec, you have traffic at 10 o'clock, westbound," scan the horizon between the left wing and nose; the nose of the airplane is 12 o'clock in ATC language, but you must allow for a crosswind's effect on your heading. Look high and low, then report your findings, either "Three-six-Quebec, no contact" or "Three-six-Quebec, I have the traffic." If you say you have the traffic, keep it in sight until it is no longer a factor, and if contact is lost before the aircraft is clear of your path, ask ATC for its position. Separation always is the pilot's responsibility in VFR conditions, and if you say you have the traffic the controller assumes you will stay clear. If you say "No contact," the controller will monitor the situation and issue updates until you spot the bogey or until he can report that it is no longer a factor. If the traffic has an encoding altimeter but is not in contact, the controller will report it as being at "Three thousand, unverified." Do not substitute the cabin speaker for your eyeballs. Maintain your own watch even while operating in a radar environment, and enlist the aid of your passengers as well.

Switching Over to the Tower

With successive heading changes, the approach controller will align you with the arrival gate as desired by the tower controller, and will tell you when to switch to the tower frequency, usually only a few miles from the runway. "Three-six-Quebec is four miles northwest of the airport, contact tower now on one-one-eight-point-four" will be a typical handoff. You will sign off with "Three-six-Quebec, going to tower" and dial up the tower frequency unless you have the luxury of two comm sets or a preset frequency storage capability. You have only to report your position, as you are being expected by the tower controller: "Downtown Tower, Cessna three-six-Quebec, four miles northwest." You will be issued a traffic sequence, such as "Number three, follow the 727 on two-mile final," unless you happen to be the only soul in the sky at that moment.

More often than not, you will be sandwiched between two jets on final approach, and it will be helpful to all concerned to maintain as much speed as possible until just before flaring out. A 120-knot final is much more neighborly than a 70-knot one at a big airport. Practice these high-speed arrivals at home and you will soon learn just how close to the threshold you can come before bleeding off power and applying drag from the flaps and gear to touch down on a chosen spot. Plan your touchdown and rollout in order to arrive at a turnoff point without tying up the runway. If no taxiway exit is handy for some distance down the runway, aim a bit long rather than putting it on the numbers, letting the aircraft roll without delay to the turnoff and clearing the runway promptly for the sake of that jet on final. A delayed touchdown also avoids wake turbulence from the heavy aircraft that just landed, by keeping you above his flight path. Remember, the ultimate authority for safe operation of the aircraft belongs with the pilot, not the controller, so don't let a request for an expedited turnoff cause you to fold up the airplane in an attempt to comply. Just do the best you can.

Upon clearing the runway, not before, switch over to Ground Control, which you should have noted on your flight log in case the tower is too busy to give you the usual "Three-six-Quebec, turn right next taxiway, point-nine clearing the runway." Again, tell the controller your ident, position, and intentions: "Downtown ground, Cessna three-six-Quebec, just cleared one-two left, taxiing to general aviation parking." For your first visit to this virgin sod, it would be well to have someone along who is familiar with the lay of the land; if this is not possible, get a good briefing on the ground layout in advance. You can solicit help from Ground Control by saying you're unfamiliar with the airport; they'll gladly lead you by the hand rather than have you blunder onto an active runway. Remember, taxiways are named for phonetic letters, such as Alpha, Delta, Romeo, etc., so you may be told "North on Delta, east on Romeo" as taxi instructions. If you're dropping off or picking up passengers, you can inform the controller "We have passengers for Continental Flight 212" in case there is a special gate for such purposes.

Getting Out Again

Departure from the TCA is even easier than arrival—simply a matter of getting a departure clearance before taxi. Listen to the ATIS first, then contact clearance delivery on the frequency specified by the ATIS recording, not Ground Control. Clearance will want to know your direction of flight and desired altitude, so you can say "Downtown clearance delivery, Cessna one-two-three-six-Quebec is requesting a clearance out of the TCA. We will be VFR northwestbound to Armonk, requesting "three thousand." Clearance delivery will then assign the transponder code, heading to fly after takeoff, and frequency on which to contact Departure Control. You enter the code in your transponder, but remain in "standby" mode on the ground. You then contact Ground Control, giving your position and intentions: "Downtown Ground Control, Cessna one-two-three-six-Quebec is at general aviation parking, ready to taxi for takeoff, we have Tango." Again, ask for taxi instructions if you're not sure of yourself, to avoid embarrassment.

After runup is complete at the end of the runway, turn on the transponder and tell the tower you're ready to go. If you are attempting to speed things up by departing from an intersection, you may be thwarted by mandatory holds due to wake turbulence from departing jets. It sometimes pays to taxi to the far end of the runway, where you have the option of waiving the hold if you feel you can avoid the turbulence.

Shortly after liftoff you will be told to "Fly heading zero-six-zero, contact Departure Control now on one-one-niner-point-three." You will check in with Departure Control as "Downtown Departure, Cessna three-six-Quebec, just off one-two left, turning to zero-six-zero." Departure will reply "Three-six-Quebec is radar contact, maintain three-thousand." Radar vectors and traffic advisories will be given in a manner similar to arrival, until you reach the outer limits of the TCA or the fringes of radar coverage. At this point you will be told "Radar service terminated, squawk VFR, resume normal navigation." You reply, "Three-six-Quebec, squawking twelve-hundred," perhaps with a word of thanks for the assistance. Be sure to clear your transponder by turning the knobs back to 1200 so you will not be squawking a discrete code that is assigned to another airplane.

As you can see, TCA entry and exit procedures are not more complicated than using radar services at a TRSA or ARSA airport. You have only to follow instructions and keep on top of the situation, complying in a professional manner with the controller's instructions. Talk clearly and concisely on the radio, as the pro pilots do, but don't be so rapid-fire with your cryptic replies that you are constantly being asked to "Say again." Laconic replies also are frowned upon, so try to strike a happy medium.

Don't fear the big airport; just behave yourself and with practice you'll find that flying into the TCA airport is almost like operating at home base.

Part III
Weather

Chapter 13
The Briefing

The pilot had been marooned by low stratus and fog for a couple of days, making frequent trips between the airport and the motel, and he had called Flight Service regularly for more weather information. I bumped into him at the airport coffee pot, and chatted sympathetically about his chances for getting out that day. I opined that the stationary front was bound to be drifting eastward soon, but a low pressure area was impeding its progress and was pumping in a southeasterly flow of moist air. His response was a bit unexpected: "Where is the low?" he asked.

Now, we've all been in this man's shoes. Trapped away from home by a stalled weather system, we desperately want to know when it's safe to plan a departure at the earliest possible moment. Yet after two days of calling the FSS regularly, this pilot didn't know the overall weather pattern. Somehow, he had never learned to brief himself, with the assistance of Flight Service.

Before You Call

To safely fly cross-country with a minimum of inconvenience, you must know as much about the weather you're faced with as the person answering the FSS phone. True, the FSS individual is a trained weather briefer, and he or she will do their best to give you what they and the briefer's manual feel is adequate information for the flight, but only *you* can decide whether it's good enough for you to go. You are a pilot; you will see more weather firsthand in a month of flying than most weather briefers will see in a decade. You should learn from each flight, and be better prepared for the next one by observing the conditions encountered.

Before calling the FSS, learn as much as possible about the overall weather situation, so you can be aware of problems and ask

Fig. 13-1. A television weather map, such as this one from *AM Weather*, gives you a basic feel for the day's conditions. Start with the "big picture" and add your observations to it when forced to create your own weather briefing.

specific questions. You should know the location of highs and lows, as well as frontal zones, and the type of air mass involved (dry, moist, polar, maritime, etc.). Thus prepared, you can ask intelligent questions of the briefer and weigh the merits of the forecasts.

Finding out the big picture isn't all that difficult; one of the best TV presentations is still the early-morning "Today" show on NBC because it's made up only an hour or two before show time. "A.M. Weather" is a pilot-oriented program on various public-television stations, also an early-morning presentation, and locally-originated TV weather shows, while varying widely in content and veracity, can be better than nothing. If you are in an area with cable TV offering the nationwide Weather Channel, originating in Atlanta, it provides aviation weather hourly. If no prior information is available, make sure you get an area synopsis from the briefer, so you can relate it to his other data.

I highly recommend the purchase of a portable low-frequency radio, with which you can listen to the TWEB (Transcribed Weather Broadcast) on the 150 to 400 kHz band practically anywhere in the country. They are not easy to buy, since most radios advertised as "weather radios" actually use the VHF public-service weather band, which is not flying weather. If you can get a radio with the VHF aircraft band, so much the better, because the LF band fills up with static during times of electrical storms and you may be able to switch over to VHF and pick up a TWEB from a nearby VOR offering it. If you have an ADF radio in your airplane it can also pick up the TWEB's LF broadcasts. The NDB or VOR will have a small, solid square in the lower right corner of its data box on the chart if it is TWEB equipped.

Now You're Ready . . .

For the most current reports of weather, call the FSS following about 10 minutes after the hour. Weather observations are taken just before the hour, and for several minutes the computers are tied up with loading in fresh reports, so calling just before the hour will get you sequences nearly an hour old, and no sequences will be available for a short period exactly on the hour. Delaying a few minutes will get you the latest poop, perhaps altering your decision. Remember, however, that sequence reports are only spot observations; they must be used in conjunction with the big picture to update the changing weather pattern. By gleaning information such as wind shifts at various stations, or changing cloud heights, you will be able to stay abreast of the situation.

Forecasts are important, naturally. They are prepared for several hours at a time, overlapping with the preceding forecasts for continuity. Area forecasts predict the changing big picture, and terminal forecasts take into account micrometeorology at specific airports, so you'll know if you can see to land after you get there. Use both, but compare forecasts diligently with reported weather to see how things are going.

When you dial up the FSS, state your aircraft number and intentions for their benefit, then request specific information, rather than casting yourself on the briefer's mercy. Where is the front now? Have you any pilot reports along my route? What was the last radar report showing on precipitation areas? Ask for reports and forecasts for the stations you feel are significant, if you don't get them as part of the standard briefing. Reporting points "upstream" in the path of weather movement can bear a clue to the conditions moving into your route during the next few hours. Learn where the good weather lies, so you can head in the proper direction if your destination is unreachable.

Above all, write down the information. You may have need of comparing the next hour's weather with this hour's to establish a trend, and unless you have a photographic memory, you won't remember the cloud heights next hour. Devise your own shorthand system if need be, but note the weather reported at each station somehow for later reference.

Analyze What You've Heard

Exactly what are you looking for in this mass of data? You want to know what the current weather is along your route, and what it is forecast to be. In most cases the forecast is already in effect, so compare actual weather with the forecast. If the forecast was for improvement, has such a trend really begun? If the situation is supposed to deteriorate, is it proceding as predicted? If improvement is slower than forecast, perhaps you shouldn't place too much faith in the forecast. On the other hand, improvement may be occurring well ahead of expectations, a welcome sign. Be especially watchful of winds that are stronger than forecast; these can indicate a low pressure system deepening or moving in sooner than expected. In such a case, all bets are off, and amended forecasts probably will be out shortly.

Should you be faced with marginal conditions, try to establish a trend over several sequence reports, and stay on the ground until an upward trend is shown over at least three hours. Check several stations, to make sure you are not dealing with a localized problem. In any case, suitable alternatives should be within easy reach before you tackle weather that pushes your limitations.

As the pilot in command, you must decide for yourself if the weather is adequate for the flight. Safe VFR is not the regulatory 1000 feet of ceiling and three miles of visibility; it is whatever ceiling and visibility will allow you a comfortable safety margin to hunt an alternative field if deteriorating conditions are encountered. Likewise, 200 feet and one-half mile are not adequate landing minima for a rusty instrument pilot. Marginal weather is defined by the limitations of your aircraft and your personal abilities, *not* by the FARs.

For the foregoing reasons, you cannot place the go /no-go decision in the hands of the FSS, asking in effect, "Is it okay if I go now?" The National Weather Service and the FAA briefers exist to bring you the information on which to base an intelligent decision. To make such a decision, you need to know as much as possible about the weather picture, and have a clear idea about what information you can get from the briefer. It's *your* neck that's at stake, not the weather briefer's.

Chapter 14

Doing Your Own Forecasting

The fifth paragraph of FAR Part 91 states that the pilot is required to check weather reports and forecasts for any flight under IFR or not in the vicinity of the airport (whatever *that* is supposed to be). Unfortunately, as general aviation's capabilities have increased, the availability of weather information has decreased, placing the IFR or cross-country pilot at a disadvantage both legally and practically. At most airports the only means of getting a weather briefing is by long-distance phone call to a faraway Flight Service Station. Assuming a phone is even available, all too often the lines are jammed.

A good weather briefing is worth its weight in gold, particularly if (pardon the pun) the situation is clouded. When there isn't a cloud in the sky and winds are light, few pilots will think twice about pushing off on a short flight without checking the weather. But when the ceiling lowers and precipitation develops, everybody wants help in determining the best course of action. It is possible to undertake a flight in the face of less-than-perfect conditions if a good weather briefing is available.

Without such a briefing, you had better stay on the ground, or at least close to an airport. A lack of current weather information limits the pilot's weather knowledge to what he can see happening around him, severely hampering the utility of today's fast, long-range airplanes. Sadly, there's always a pilot or two who is unwilling to accept the stark facts seen through his windshield, weather briefing or not. We read about them all too often in the newspapers. The solution to weather-related accidents is twofold: 1) Learn to be your own weather prophet, and 2) Stay within the limitations prescribed by the reliability of your weather data.

Knowing What to Watch For

The best weather information often is not available from the FSS. The pilot who just landed can tell you more than any briefer, assuming he is observant enough to recall temperature, cloud height, and drift angles. Get the word from someone who just covered the proposed route and you'll have a better handle on what to expect. Of course, the situation can change in the course of a flight, so temper the pilot's report with your own observations and intuition.

As in the preceding section, get a general synopsis of the weather picture from some source. This information is particularly valuable if you're forced to make up your own forecast. A TV weather map can give you an idea of the positions of highs and lows, as well as the major fronts; from this you judge circulation patterns and possible cloud types.

If a low is moving in, expect a general worsening of weather conditions before an improvement starts and a counterclockwise circulation of winds and weather around the low center. If the winds are strong, the low center is probably close by, and if moisture is available to create clouds and saturate the air, flying may be chancey. A nice fat high, on the other hand, will provide a reasonable guarantee of good flying weather, barring such problems as upslope lifting of moisture, which can form low status, or high winds generated by a rapid pressure change.

Fronts may or may not spell trouble, but they must be viewed with at least a cautious eye. If the front is dry, the boundary between air masses might be marked by only a little turbulence and a few scattered clouds. If there is available moisture being fed to the front by strong winds, the stability of the air mass behind the front becomes highly volatile, generating thunderstorms. The more common cold front is a fast-moving, violent thrust into a warm, moist air mass, with a narrow band or two of thunderstorms associated with the front. If the warm air sector pushes into the cold air mass as a warm front, you can be just as effectively grounded by widespread low stratus and drizzle. Fronts, like low pressure areas, should be considered a potential threat to your plans, so know the big picture before you attempt to make up your own forecast.

What's Happening Overhead?

After obtaining an overview of the weather situation take a look at the sky condition, discounting any local pollution. Hazy visibilities obviously mean moisture is present in the air, probably with little temperature decrease at altitude or maybe an inversion (warming with altitude). Haze is not only a hazard to navigation, it is a potential weather-maker if a strong push of cold air enters the warm, moist air. In weak weather systems, you may find isolated afternoon thunderstorms sitting in the middle of the haze, even if there is no well-defined front.

An absence of clouds, with blue, haze-free skies, probably means a cold front has passed through recently; if you're heading in the direction of its movement you might delay your departure a few hours to let it move well ahead, then you're probably home free. The presence of a high, thin overcast and some lower clouds could mean that you're on borrowed time; the clear skies are past and another weather system is moving in, probably in 12 hours or less. If you're spending the night, be prepared to make an early departure if you want to run ahead of the weather or a delayed one if you plan to push on after it passes.

Observing weather movement day after day soon will teach you the basic signals; wispy cirrus tells of approaching weather 12 to 24 hours before it arrives, middle-layer clouds start to gather under the cirrus overcast a few hours in advance of the weather, and ground-hugging stratus crowds in as the low center approaches, assuming enough moisture is present. A low stratus deck obscures your view of the sky, of course, and in this case you will have to get an on-top report from an IFR pilot who has penetrated the fog layer. If he says there's nothing but clear sky above the low layer, you will probably have no weather problem after the fog lifts.

Winds and Weather

The velocity of the winds aloft tells you how soon to expect a change in the weather. If the winds are stronger than suspected, any forecast you have heard had best be accelerated. Observe the movement of low or middle-layer clouds to detect a strong low-level airflow. If only cirrus clouds are visible, note whether they are arranged in streamers, or "mare's tails," due to the strong winds in the upper atmosphere. Wind is weather, as far as pilots are concerned, particularly in mountainous areas; wind always determines the rate of weather change. Wind is movement of air from a high-pressure peak to fill a low-pressure depression. The stronger the wind, the more intense the pressure change will be and the more violent the accompanying weather, depending on the amount of moisture available.

Cloud types affect your flying decisions, of course. Cumulus clouds mean vertical air movement, so you can expect to find turbulence below their bases, forcing you to climb high to seek a smooth ride. A stratus overcast that blocks the sun's heating can assure a good ride at all levels, but if the clouds are thick enough to be a solid layer there may be a low center nearby, collecting the clouds, so you should be alert for lowering ceilings as you fly toward the low. Low scud is definitely a no-go situation unless you're instrument-rated and have enough fuel to make a run for good weather.

How do you judge cloud height? Even the best of us get fooled, but with practice you can learn to gauge a ceiling by watching for such clues as movement in the cloud layer and fragments of clouds. If you can actually see the cloud layer being pushed along rapidly by the winds aloft, the bases probably are very low or the winds are very high. Little or no movement and an inability to detect individual cloud fragments probably means several thousand feet lie between you and the cloud base. A pilot report is the best guide to cloud height unless you want to take a sounding yourself. Beware of "taking a look" if the surface visibility is low; the bases may be only a few hundred feet above the ground, adding moisture to reduce visibility and making even a traffic-pattern flight hazardous.

Turbulence

A pilot needs to know a little about the characteristics of the air mass he's observing in order to assess the probability of a smooth flight. Unfortunately, most low-flying VFR pilots prefer to fly in conditions that have the potential for being turbulent. The clear or nearly-cloudless blue of the first day following a cold front's passage is advertised as being stable air, but the ride down low is liable to be as rough as a washboard. Below the condensation level, marked by the bases of the puffs of fair weather cumulus, the cold air is being warmed by ground radiation and is reabsorbing moisture deposited by the frontal storms, and thermals will be booming up everywhere. Smooth air at low altitudes, by comparison, will more than likely be stagnate, filled with moisture and pollution, which reduces visibility, a by-product of the air's inability to generate strong vertical currents.

If you take note of the temperature at various altitudes, you'll find that a rapid cooling as you ascend often accompanies clear skies, while haze conditions are usually associated with a flat or inverted temperature gradient. If the free-air temperature warms with altitude, then suddenly begins to cool, you'll probably find yourself entering clear air above the haze layer, as the haze ends at the top of the temperature inversion.

The FAA would seem to be bent on serving only major metropolitan areas with current weather information, as more and more facilities are being remoted and FSS stations are closed, so when you're stuck in Pumpkin Center, where even calling the county seat requires a toll charge, you may have trouble getting an FSS briefing even by phone. I have often seen pilots try for 15 minutes to reach the FSS when the phone lines are tied up to the briefers, listening to a recording of "All briefers are busy, please stand by . . ." If you're forced to make up your own forecast in an out-of-the-way place, consider the big picture you should always have in your mind, listen to transcribed weather on the ADF or VOR radio, check with pilots arriving, and apply your acquired weather wisdom. Above all, don't push your luck beyond your definite knowledge of the weather. The best insurance is still a good weather briefing . . . if you can just get one.

Chapter 15

Coping with Marginal VFR

"What am I doing here?" was my frequent thought as I feverishly tried to compare the limited view of the landscape with my Sectional Chart. I was a freshly minted commercial pilot, a downy-cheeked 200-hour wonder, back in the days when instrument ratings were for airline pilots. I was off on my first charter trip, slogging my way across the trackless prairie in pouring rain laced with lightning bolts. The paying customer beside me wasn't overly concerned, not realizing the difference between an airplane and a car as far as ease of navigation was concerned. For my part, I was ready to pull over to the side of the road and hole up for a while, but the last airport was a half-hour back and I really wasn't all that sure where the next reachable one might be.

As often happens, the god in charge of looking after fools that day permitted the rain to moderate in time for me to orient myself and find the destination, which I thought at the time was due to some pretty neat flying on my part. It was even legal VFR weather, as near as I can remember, because I was quick to duck below 1200 feet AGL when the visibility dropped below three miles; it wasn't that I was concerned with technicalities, I just wanted to stay within sight of the buffalo chips.

Somehow, selling aviation has always bordered on fraud. We tempt a non-pilot with stories of how we made it from Chicago to Nashville in three hours, never telling about the three days it took to get back home. Mostly, we're inclined to forget about the trips that didn't run on schedule and remember only the uneventful ones that wafted us above the mere earthbound mortals with our seven-league boots. As wives and business associates soon learn, an airplane is not a flying automobile; a pilot's word is worthless when weather intervenes. The brochures always feature shiny new airplanes winging through clear blue skies, carrying jubilant occupants to always-VFR destinations. Like the song says, I learned the truth at seventeen; it 'tain't always like that.

Far from abandoning the VFR airplane as a tool of transportation, we need only to face reality and make plans for disruption in our schedule. It is quite possible to fly under less than tourist-folder weather conditions, providing we don't try to keep *every* appointment and fly *every* trip. Even as an instrument pilot, you aren't going to do that—at least not if you're smart.

Rules for Survival

Rule One is *Stay flexible; if you can't go now, go later.* If you can't get through the pass, go around the hills. He who *has* to get through eventually gets killed trying; the pilot wise enough to wait a few hours might have a relatively easy trip. Timing can be everything. The really low scud may only be down on the deck for a couple of hours, but if those are the two hours in which you make your attempt, you'll never know what you missed. Go when you can, not when you feel you must. Most business or family appointments can slide a half-day and those that can't require alternate travel plans to cover the weather's vagaries.

Rule Two is *Believe only what you see in the windshield.* Sure, you're going to get a weather briefing, for all the good that does. Sometimes the briefer knows less than you do, so use the FSS as it was intended—for weather information, not decisions. *You* make the decisions because it is *your* tail that gets busted. I had a briefer tell me it was "marginal VFR" last week. He didn't know I had been copying recorded weather for the past three hours, so I asked him where it was "marginal VFR" as forecast. He searched the sequences, and concluded that one station 250 miles away had 1400 overcast with seven miles, so the "marginal VFR" was far from widespread and the area forecast was overly pessimistic. On the other hand, a trip the following week was briefed to be a good VFR joyride only to conclude in an instrument approach.

Rule Three is *Use what you have available.* A VOR airway is nice to follow in flat country, but not worth a darn in the hills when you have to stay low. A railroad track makes a dandy courseline if it's the only one in the country, but it's a poor one in a metropolitan area. Holding a compass heading in hopes of finding a landmark or a VOR can be a ticket to nowhere if the effect of a strong crosswind is not anticipated.

Rule Four is *Never shut the door behind you.* Have an airport at your back at all times, or one in the direction of good weather. I only like to gamble on a sure thing and the weather doesn't fit those odds. Have somewhere to go when Mother Nature fools you. The statement "Sure was lucky this airport was here" should mean "This airport was right where I planned for it to be, in case the weather turned out as it did."

Define Marginal VFR

What's marginal VFR, anyway? To the FSS specialist, it's a ceiling of less than 3000 feet or visibility of less than five miles. To the layman aviator, it's any weather that makes him or her uncomfortable, and sometimes it takes a lot less than the aforementioned FSS parameters. When it's after sundown, that 3000-and-five weather is nowhere near our real VFR requirements, and if we're heading toward rising terrain, even in broad daylight, we want more than 3000 feet of clearance reported down here in the valley. The first trip into an area also requires a little better weather than one could comfortably handle after gaining familiarity with the locale. A 30-mile trip creates less sweat than a 300-mile one. We might not even need a 1000-foot ceiling to find our way home when we're only ten minutes out from the airport.

Now, of course, we're going to avoid flying marginal VFR

Fig. 15-1. Now, *this* is marginal VFR! Dropping down a bit to clearer air below the cloud base may help, but you must set limits on how low you will go. Keep an alternative always in mind!

weather conditions intentionally. But there will be times when the forecast misses or unknown pockets of low weather are encountered. In these cases, your marginal-VFR flying skills had better be up to snuff. Plan your flight with the possibility of coping with rotten weather; be ready to abandon the direct route or VOR airway, relying instead on a major highway, railroad track, or waterway that will take you where you want to go. Stick closer to airports when the weather lowers; these escape sanctuaries will be more numerous along highways, railroads and rivers. You may never actually have to make a diversion to your low-visibility route, but it's nice to have it planned.

Use all means at your disposal to learn about the weather ahead. As always, know the big picture, so you can turn the right way to find better conditions when your route gets clobbered. Keep up with hourly sequence reports using Flight Watch, FSS, or the transcribed weather reports available from VOR or NDB stations charted with a small solid square in the right lower corner of their identification block. Ask Unicom stations 25 miles or so ahead how their weather looks; the line person may not be a weather expert but he or she will know if it's raining or fogged in. Pass pilot reports along to FSS as you reach each VOR station to help the chap coming along behind you.

Giving Up Gracefully

When do you chicken out? Whenever you're having difficulty seeing checkpoints and staying clear of clouds. Stay in firm ground contact, descending immediately or making a 180° turn when you run into scud at or below your flight level. It's amazing how much better the visibility becomes with a few hundred feet of clearance below the cloud base. The legal 500 feet is little enough for good forward visibility. Even if you're IFR rated, don't try to scud-run just to put off seeking a clearance—there could be rocks in those clouds. If you can legally file for an instrument clearance, get onto a route segment that will keep you safely above all obstructions. Don't wander into the clouds in anticipation of a vector.

Set definite limits on how low you will go. An altitude of 1000 feet AGL is beginning to get right down on the deck, and three miles of visibility is about the least one should attempt, even in flat country, with a modern two-mile-a-minute airplane. It is best to start planning early, looking over the options when you are pressed down to 1500 feet AGL, and consider a diversion rather strongly at 1200 feet AGL. Definitely execute a 180 or deviation to the alternate route when pressed down to 1000 feet AGL. If you're on a good pilotage route, such as a highway, the temptation is strong to keep going, even down to 500 feet AGL. This is foolhardy; if the weather has deteriorated to that degree already, it will very likely continue to do so. It's time to head for the barn, so don't attempt suicide by continuing on.

A sliding scale of ceiling and visibility values is useful for the VFR pilot. Don't plan on giving up both ceiling and visibility. Three miles of hazy visibility isn't so bad in familiar country with no clouds overhead, but it's pretty chancey under a 1000-foot overcast. On the other hand, a 1000-foot ceiling could be safely negotiated with 25 miles of visibility underneath and no higher terrain ahead, but even five to seven miles is little enough when the clouds start dropping. Knowledge of the area, the type of terrain, and the availability of alternate routes should influence your decision to continue or land at an alternate.

Above all, don't crowd your capabilities in marginal VFR weather. It's all right to drop down and go a little farther when the clouds thicken up, as long as you have an alternate escape route planned and the firm resolve to call it quits when you reach your preset minimums. Just make that 180° turn before you go too far.

Chapter 16

When You're Trapped in IFR Weather

You're a VFR pilot; your license reads Airplane, Single-Engine Land, period. But you've probably had enough instrument time to feel capable of flying in the clouds for brief periods. Think again. As envisioned by the drafters of the FARs, the basic VFR pilot's level of instrument competence is sufficient to make a 180° turn into clear air or negotiate a letdown without falling into a graveyard spiral. By no means are VFR-only pilots supposed to head intentionally into a cloud deck.

Suppose, however, that you are heading cross-country and are flying through steadily deteriorating conditions. Because you want to get to your destination, you continue. This leads inevitably to pushing on too far, and sooner or later you'll say to yourself, "How do I get myself out of this mess?"

Start by reasoning out how you got *into* it. Weather doesn't trap pilots; pilots trap themselves by ignoring danger signs and not preparing for possible changes in conditions. You saw the weather develop as you flew toward it, and as a VFR pilot you should be flying in relatively good weather only. Therefore, the way out is the way back. You don't *want* to turn around, but do you want to keep forging ahead badly enough to die trying?

The High Road, and the Low Road

Of course, there is always a possibility of getting out of the clouds by going up or down. Exercising this option requires that the decision be made before the troublesome cloud deck solidifies, since you are required to maintain a 2000-foot cloud separation as you penetrate the layer. As the breaks will become fewer and smaller, you had best make your move early. Going on top can sometimes seem safe and easy as the beautiful vista of clear blue sky and

Fig. 16-1. Clouds, cloud everywhere, and not a hole in sight. A VFR pilot in this situation had better start working on an escape plan. If an instrument letdown is needed, be sure you're equal to the task.

snow-white clouds lulls one into a sense of security. One still has to navigate, however, which means relying on VOR or ADF signals unless the breaks in the clouds are numerous; VFR pilots may not be used to the regimen of blind navigation. There's also a chance of getting trapped between two cloud layers coming together as one nears a low-pressure center.

Going on top involves a gamble by the VFR pilot that things will open up or at least get no worse as he approaches the destination. That gamble doesn't always pay off, resulting in a long on-top retreat with diminishing fuel reserves, looking for a hole. You'll have to get down sometime, and without an instrument rating, equipment, and currency, you must do it VFR.

Dropping down, to go under, is a good option if you want to maintain ground contact, but you may encounter reduced visibility under the cloud deck and you'll probably be subjected to more turbulence. You'll have to abide by definite limits on how low you can go, depending on terrain and obstructions ahead. Navigation by pilotage is easy, but radio reception for VOR tracking is compromised by the low flight level. It's easier to reach an airport in a hurry by staying under the clouds, one positive aspect of taking the low road.

But you've now tried too hard, and you're really in it. You can't see the ground except for an occasional glimpse, and this cloud doesn't seem to be "just another little puff" like you'd hoped. You've gotten yourself into a bad situation, and now you've got to get yourself out. Avoid panic at all costs; grabbing the mike and hollering for help won't bring somebody to take over the controls. Fly the airplane first, and in due course you can ask for assistance.

As If Your Life Depended on It

Concentrate on keeping the wings level, using the top index of the artificial horizon. Relax the death-grip on the control yoke, or you'll first climb, then over-react with a dive. The nose of the airplane belongs on the horizon bar, but remember it'll tend to go there by itself if you'll just relax and let the trim tab do its job. Now that you know how to stay upright, look at the upside-down number on the bottom of the directional gyro and begin a turn; roll out on that heading. Ignore the directional gyro for a minute or so, as you won't need it, and concentrate instead on flying the artificial horizon to stay in a 15° to 20° bank with the noise level.

You don't have one of those newfangled full-face DGs? Well, you can add 200 to your present heading and subtract 20, which turns 115° into 295°, or take away 200 and add 20 if your heading is already past 200°. If that's too much to handle, just hold the bank at 15° to 20° for one minute, then roll out, and you will be close to a 180° change in direction in the average lightplane.

After completing the 180° turn, hold the wings level and stay on your chosen heading. You are now on the way to the better weather you left behind, and a few minutes of straight and level flight will probably bring improved conditions. If it doesn't, you can begin a cautious letdown, as long as you are reasonably aware of your location and can estimate a safe level-off altitude, so you won't penetrate a mountain peak. Should you be unsure of your position in a mountainous area, you'll have no choice but to climb until reaching an altitude that will clear the terrain. Then you may as well confess your emergency and get help to find your way down.

If a descent is called for, reduce power 300-400 rpm in airplanes with a fixed-pitch propeller, or 4-5 inches of mp if you have a constant-speed prop. Allow the nose to drop below the horizon until the attitude gyro's horizon bar rests on the top of the artificial airplane's nose dot or gull wings. This should yield about a 500-fpm descent rate at cruise speed, with no trim change required; keep the wings level, don't apply back pressure, and wait for the ground to appear. Try to form some idea of how low you can go and still have

500 feet or so of terrain clearance; be ready to abandon the descent in case you're in an area of zero-zero fog. Because you're heading back toward better weather, you'll most likely break out after a few hundred feet of descent. Remember to level off at least 500 feet below the cloud base, so you'll not only be legal but will benefit from improved visibility as you remove yourself from the moisture.

When All Else Fails . . .

Now for the worst possibility: You've turned around, descended, given up and climbed, all without seeing anything but cloud. Survival now depends on keeping a clear head and confessing your predicament. I realize the standard recommendations for VFR pilots trapped in weather are to climb immediately and ask for assistance, but making a 180° turn and letting down can often eliminate the need for ATC help, if action is taken promptly. Never forget who has to fly the airplane; if you seek ground assistance you'll still be the one who has to hold a heading and stay upright.

But if you don't see any other way out, get help to find the way down. While maintaining a heading, turn up the volume and open the squelch on the radio. Dial in an FSS frequency and attempt to contact Flight Service. They won't have ATC radar, but they can refer you to someone who does. Just give them your call sign, general location, and frequency on which you're listening. If you're requesting a reply on the VOR frequency, don't forget to turn up both volume knobs, nav as well as comm. After you get a reply, confess your situation and ask for assistance in getting back to better weather. If you don't get a reply, you may need to climb higher to establish line-of-sight contact with the ground station's antenna. If all attempts at communication fail, your best course of action is to track inbound toward a navigation station along your general route of flight and try again later. Your preflight preparations should have included forming a mental picture of where blue sky lay so you would know which way to head if things got really bad. However, you probably omitted this step or you wouldn't be in this mess now.

If the situation is urgent, go directly to 121.5, the emergency channel, which could save a few minutes while FSS looks up a Center frequency for you. You can, of course, call up Center yourself if you have the frequency available. Be prepared to follow instructions and answer questions when you establish communications with an ATC controller. He'll want to know your aircraft type, number of persons on board, and hours of fuel remaining. You'll also be asked if you're instrument qualified and equipped; you'll have to answer in the negative, so you'll be asked if you want to declare an emergency, unless the controller wishes to assume the obvious—that a VFR pilot in the clouds *is* an emergency. You may as well declare; if you had any other choice, you wouldn't be calling ATC.

For Emergency Use Only

When an emergency situation has been declared, the rulebook can be discarded and you can get priority handling to conclude your emergency as quickly as possible. Expect identification procedures, in the form of a transponder code or identifying turn, so you'll be easier to see on radar. If you used 7700, the transponder code for emergency, you'll probably be pulled off that code after communications are established.

If radar identification is made, if you can fly the airplane well enough to hold a heading, and if you're not low on fuel, it should be simple for ATC to direct you to an area with higher ceilings and away from instrument traffic, where you can let down into the clear and land with no more emergencies. The controller would prefer to keep you in firm radar contact, so he'll probably try to hold you above a certain altitude for tracking purposes until you're near the field. Don't argue about his choice of airports; cooperate by getting on the ground and ending the emergency for everyone.

In case you are having difficulty handling the airplane and keeping up with the controller's barrage of instructions and questions, don't be afraid to speak up and tell him you're having trouble with the airplane. Remember, you are receiving assistance from the ATC system, but it can't fly the airplane for you.

After your encounter with IFR weather is over, whether it involved a contact with ATC or just a few seconds of sweaty palms while you escaped the fog, take a cold, hard look at how you got there so you won't let it happen again. Doing something dumb can serve a purpose if you are honest enough to tell yourself "Hey, that was stupid." Be sure you find a way to avoid making the same mistake twice. Review your weather briefing technique, and get with an instructor to talk it over. You may not get another chance to mend your ways.

Part IV
Surviving the Seasons

Chapter 17
Wisdom for a
Windy Spring Day

It was a day fit only for the hardy and the half-witted. The wind sock snapped to and fro, trees sighed as their branches bent with the wind's force, and little airplanes rocked nervously in their tiedowns. Pilots who succeeded in landing their aircraft offloaded ashen-faced passengers and told of encountering "severe turbulence" aloft. Clearly, it was no day to go flying . . . or, was it?

Perhaps a rough, windy day isn't the most comfortable time to be flying, but it can provide a chance to improve your flying skills. If you want to grow as a pilot, you must treat everything as an opportunity, including some rough air now and then. The number of accidents resulting from loss of directional control during takeoff and landing leads us to believe that pilots aren't staying sharp on their runway handling, probably because more and more airplanes are being used for transportation, an application that provides few takeoffs and landings to maintain proficiency.

So, if you want to stay sharp, take advantage of this gusty afternoon and fly a few circuits in preparation for the day when you get caught in just such conditions while coming in with a load of passengers. It isn't possible to avoid all encounters with strong winds, and if you pass up this chance to practice you'll be just that much more rusty when the inevitable showdown comes.

How Much Wind Is Too Much?

Two limitations are placed on our operations, that of the airplane and that of the pilot. No matter how well-designed the airplane, some recently licensed or rusty pilots are just not qualified to fly in winds of more than 15 knots, at least not until they gain more experience by flying in progressively stronger winds. On the other hand, even the best pilot can't handle a wind that exceeds the airplane's ability to provide control. Such control limits are usually reached during crosswind operations, either on the runway or while taxiing. For a rough rule of thumb, figure on running into difficulty whenever the wind speed is greater than one-half the airplane's stalling speed, so if your bird has a 60-knot V_{so}, operating in winds of 30 knots will be stretching the airplane's limits, even if the wind sock is pointing straight down the runway.

Another axiom that has kept me out of trouble on many an occasion states that "If you can't taxi, don't fly." When the wind is so strong that you have difficulty holding the airplane straight while taxiing, or if the gusts tend to lift a wheel off the ground, forget it—put 'er back in the shed and wait for a better day. The use of brakes to control one's taxi path is not unusual in tailwheel aircraft, but most nosewheel-equipped airplanes shouldn't be operated in winds strong enough to require brakes for directional control. (The exceptions are those planes with full-castering nosegear, such as the Grumman singles.)

Even if you observe those two limitations, there will be plenty of days when the winds are strong enough to make you wish you were somewhere else. However, you won't learn anything by leaving the airplane in the tiedowns and only flying it on perfectly calm days. Practice, even if only for a half-hour or so, hones your skills for that day when the winds pick up while you are enroute. There are pilots and there are passengers; make sure the person sitting in the left front seat of your airplane is a *pilot*, ready to handle any and all flight conditions.

Plan for the Worst

Undertaking a bit of windy-day practice requires some forethought, such as checking the forecasts to see how strong the winds are supposed to get (maybe they haven't peaked out yet). Other runways should be available, in case the wind shifts or the currently acceptable crosswind component increases. The alternate runways need not be on the departure airport, but they should be nearby, well within range of the fuel supply.

How do you determine the wind's speed? If a tower, FSS, or Unicom is on the field, you can always ask the controller or station operator for a wind check, but if a ground observer's report is not available, other methods will do. A large wind sock will generally fill to a straight-out position with approximately 25 knots of wind; drooped to a 45° angle, the sock will signify winds of 10-15 knots. Twenty-five knots are also indicated if the trees are tossing their branches about briskly; if entire trees are swaying before the gale, you are probably experiencing a 35-knot wind. If you are within sight of a lake or river, 15 knots of wind will generate a few whitecaps, and 25 knots will produce whitecaps over most of the surface, probably with wavetops blowing spray downwind. At 35 knots, windstreaks of foam will be seen moving across the water.

Taxi slowly as you move out to go practice; the greater the wind, the slower the taxi speed needed. Use minimum power and brakes during taxi so the airplane will not lean downwind on sharp corners. Hold your controls properly to keep the wings and tail from being lifted by the wind; if taxiing upwind, hold the stick slightly aft of neutral (full aft for tailwheels), and if a crosswind component exists, hold the ailerons full into the wind. Taxiing downwind, the stick goes full forward with ailerons held away from the crosswind. If you can't remember control positions, just look at the ailerons and elevators and imagine the position that will keep the wind from "getting under" the airplane and lifting it. In this way, you can see the benefit of keeping the elevators and the windward aileron deflection down in a tailwind, directing the wind over airplane rather than under it.

Assuming you arrive at the end of the runway without undue difficulty, park with the airplane headed into the wind to avoid damage from control surfaces being slammed to the stops, as well as for improved engine cooling and better stability when you increase power for the run-up.

The Windy Traffic Pattern

After the checkout, line up carefully for the takeoff. If there is a crosswind component, begin the takeoff run with full aileron held into the wind. Maintain nosewheel contact for steering during the takeoff, but do so without putting excessive loads on the nosegear. Accelerate to a speed that will assure an immediate liftoff into a climb, then rotate the nose and "jump" into the air. Be prepared for a short takeoff roll—the airspeed indicator needle will move off the peg almost as soon as the throttle is opened.

Once off the ground and climbing, it's just like any other day, except for the turbulence buffeting the airplane. Unless there is visible evidence of an end to convective currents in the form of flat-bottomed puffs of cumulus, don't expect to be able to climb above the rough air. When surface winds reach 30 knots, moderate turbulence may extend to over 7000 feet AGL.

Someone will have to land this bucking, bouncing airplane, so there's no point in postponing the inevitable. Let not your heart be

Fig. 17-1. The crosswind is not going to upset this pilot, who is making sure he maintains runway alignment while touching down on his upwind wheel.

troubled, as the saying goes, just have a plan to keep from bending the airplane. Have your throttle hand at the ready to provide either a blast of power to arrest a sudden sink or full power to initiate a go-around. One can always go-around when the situation becomes unsalvagable, and knowing that you have such an out will prevent undue concern from interfering with your flying. Don't fret about the wind, just go around if you can't handle it and give it another try. After several unsuccessful attempts to land, proceed elsewhere and land on a runway more directly aligned into the wind or at an airport with fewer burble-generating obstructions. Even a landing in a pasture is better than creaming the airplane, if it offers an into-the-wind touchdown.

By arriving at the touchdown at just the right moment, you can sometimes catch a lull in the wind and effect a fairly normal landing even after successive go-arounds, another reason to make several attempts. It is well to land using as little flap as the runway length will permit. Some airplanes have a stalling speed several knots higher with the flaps up and the increased speed at touchdown can mean better control will be available through the landing. When stall speed is nearly the same with flaps up or down, find out which configuration gives best control and visibility in the touchdown attitude.

The touchdown should be made on the main gear with the nosewheel well clear of the runway. There is no need to try for a full-stall landing on a windy day; sacrificing control by holding off too long can lead to trouble. The best technique is to place the airplane in a slightly nose-high attitude a foot or so above the pavement, then just hold the attitude as ground contact is made. After the airplane settles on, continue flying the controls through the rollout by applying additional aileron into the wind and maintaining runway alignment with rudder. Keeping the nosegear in light but positive contact with the surface aids steering. Counter heavy brake application with up elevator to keep the main wheels in contact. Relax only when you've got the ropes tied to the wings, as the old-timers say.

A windy day is no cause for panic, although the pilot's workload is certainly increased by the challenge of the gusts. Make it a point to go out and do battle with the wind occasionally, just so you will be prepared to do some serious flying when the sock is straight out.

Chapter 18

Thunderstorms: Summer Monsters

Practically everyone knows that you just don't mix airplanes with thunderstorms. Failing to stay clear of these anvil-headed monsters has brought many an airman to grief, leaving his widow to make the best of things. The stock advice is not to take off on a cross-country flight when the route forecast includes the likelihood of thunderstorms.

Unfortunately, this advice is too all-encompassing to be realistic. Before long, a low-time pilot (known as the 200-hour menace in insurance circles) will observe other pilots coming in from a route he has just cancelled out, and they will tell him it was an easy trip, just bumpy with scattered showers. After a few of these experiences, there will come a time when he decides to take off anyway, in the face of a T-storm forecast, and he too makes it through without incident. Henceforth, he will discount any and all warnings about possible thunderstorm activity, and will continue to press his luck until he either gets the living daylights scared out of him or makes the papers.

The fact of the matter is that there aren't too many long trips that can be flown in the summer months without encountering an area where conditions are right for thunderstorm formation. To keep you aware of this, the weather service will probably issue a forecast that includes "Chance of a few scattered afternoon thunderstorms, occasionally becoming severe or forming into broken lines." The storms may not occur, or may not affect your particular flight, but the chance of you successfully making the trip depends on many factors, some of which are not under your control.

First, as in any weather situation, know the big picture, so that you can deviate slightly to avoid the worst activity. Next, try to find out the type of condition spawning the Cb development; are the storms popping up at random in an unstable air mass, or are they associated with a frontal system? Seek information about where the storms are currently located, if any, and which way they are moving.

Deciding whether or not to attempt the flight in the face of a "possible thunderstorm" forecast also depends on the difficulty of the route and the type of options available. If there are few airports along the way, if unfamiliar or rugged terrain prevails, or if other weather considerations are already chancey (poor visibility, ridges obscured), you had best not try threading your way among the miles-high storms. Certainly if the route forecast reads in such stronger terms as "moderate to severe thunderstorms likely, forming in broken to solid lines," your time would be better spend seeing to the snugness of your tiedowns.

On the other hand, if the flight is not too long, is over easy country, and is otherwise uncontaminated by weather, a cautious attempt might be possible. If you can see no towering cloud tops in the distance, in haze-free air, you ought to be good for 50 miles of exploration. A haze layer necessitates a climb to get on top of the smog before a good visual assessment can be made. Departure timing is all-important; a route open for one pilot can be completely blocked to someone coming through an hour later.

At this point, some discussion of thunderstorm theory might be in order. The cumulonimbus cloud grows in stages, first as a small popcorn-shaped cumulus, then rapidly gaining height and size until rain begins to fall. Dissipation occurs as the rain continues, the entire cycle elapsing in a span of one to three hours. Other storms develop during this time, of course, making the life cycle of a single storm rather academic to the stranded aviator.

Lifting of unstable, moisture-laden air is the act that triggers the thunderstorm formation. This lifting can be started by thermal heating, by an overriding of warm, moist air over a cold layer, or by air being pushed up a slope of a mountain range. Whatever the initial cause of lifting, under the proper conditions the warm moist air continues to rise on its own, building skyward past the condensation level where cloud forms. The rising current of air continues to carry more warm air up, building the tops higher and higher.

Eventually the moisture-laden air reaches saturation, raindrops form and begin to fall, and the Cu-type cloud changes to a mature Cb. Typically, the building cumulus stage contains updrafts while the mature storm carries both strong updrafts and downdrafts in close horizontal proximity. This severe wind shear can overstress an airplane, if the pilot does not lose control in the chaos of the storm

Fig. 18-1. This building cumulus cloud is already well above our altitude and will soon be a thunderstorm. Circumnavigation is the only safe option.

and tear it apart himself. Naturally, thunderstorms are the home of other goodies such as hail, heavy icing, lightning, and even tornadoes . . . no wonder we are told to stay clear!

How to Handle Them Inflight

How clear should you stay? From a single, moderate storm, perhaps five miles would be adequate, while a big severe storm deserves a ten-mile berth. Beware the clear sky beneath the overhanging anvil, way up there; hail often falls through this area, as the storm leans over in the upper-atmosphere winds. The point of the anvil indicates the direction of the storm's movement, if you can see it. Middle-layer clouds and building cumulus can obscure your view of the big Cb, lurking in the darkening haze ahead.

If a decision must be made about flying IFR, don't. An instrument clearance is of scant help when coping with thunderstorm avoidance, unless you have the performance to get on top of the lower cumulus and have a cooperative controller. Without radar on board as well as on the ground, your best option would be to stay at an altitude below the cloud bases, where you can see the rain areas falling from the biggies, and can hunt an airport quickly if the situation becomes untenable.

Air mass thunderstorms are frequently isolated and well scattered, and pose little problem other than an increase in fuel burn due to circumnavigation. An early start helps as the instability of the whole witches' brew increases as the sun begins to beat down. Your best trick is to be headed away from the unstable air into another airmass type, or be tied down before midafternoon.

Frontal and Orographic Storms

Frontal storms can be troublesome, depending on one's direction of flight. They are generally bigger, meaner, and have a greater tendency to hold hands when aligned with a cold front. If your route parallels the front, you may be a witness to one of nature's most spectacular displays, without becoming a participant, as you fly several hundred miles uneventfully. But you won't be able to reach a destination 20 miles away, if it happens to lie on the other side of the storm line. When tempted to break through a small gap in a line of storms, remember that more than one line of storms may precede the actual front, and you may be in worse trouble if you enter that devil's doorway to be encircled by storms. You want five miles of distance between you and the storms on each side, and a clear view of an unlimited horizon on the other side, before penetrating the line. Cold frontal storms generally move rapidly along the front itself,

Fig. 18-2. From a distance, these air-mass storms are beautiful, but they are getting too close together for a comfortable flight through their area. The anvil head of the right-hand storm is typical of a mature CB and indicates the direction of movement. The vertical lines at the top of the picture are window reflections.

from south to north, while the entire system drifts slowly eastward.

Orographic, or upslope, storms form against the windward side of a mountain range, making them a real problem if they take root in the only passes available near your route. If you are approaching from downwind of the ridgeline, you may cross it to find a valley full of violent storms, so be ready to retreat. Do not attempt to fly under the cloud bases, as upslope storms frequently shroud the higher terrain of the peak in rain and stratus.

The Great Plains of the country's midsection spawn some of the most widespread thunderstorm activity, providing an unobstructed flat region where cool Canadian and Pacific air masses can crash headlong into damp Gulf air. The results can be lines of storms stretching across several states, building up to 60,000 feet, with wind gusts to 100 mph in squall lines, and an occasional tornado. If you have a chance to see this sort of weather coming, you aren't likely to tackle it.

Reviewing the Basic Rules

Basic rules for flying in or near thunderstorm areas include staying in VFR conditions and not flying into any rain showers that you can't see a horizon beyond. Even torrential rains seldom affect the engine's performance, but poor visibility spells instrument conditions and a possible loss of control in turbulence. More importantly, you have no idea what lies beyond the obscuring rain showers, and entering that wall of water might take you into a trap of encircling thunderstorms. Don't accept just a peek of sunlight through a gap in the rain shafts—it could be the sun shining down a "chimney" in the middle of a solid mass of cells. You want a good horizon line with visible ground features as assurance of open skies beyond, and even then remember to keep miles between you and the storms as you fly through a gap. Narrow openings in a line have a way of closing up as you near or enter them, and once through it would be nice to be able to back out, should the prospects beyond the gap not be attractive.

For inflight help, ask Flight Watch for updated radar reports, which give you an idea of the size, coverage and movement of major precipitation areas. With this information, at least you will not head blindly into a worse situation. The frequency 122.0 can be a convenient listening post for information being given to other pilots, even if you don't call in yourself.

Above all, never proceed into thunderstorm areas without a clear avenue of escape to an airport, because conditions can worsen rapidly. Keeping one eye on what's going on behind you or in the direction of your "out" is vital to avoid the unpleasant and possibly fatal task of penetrating a thunderstorm in an attempt to escape your entrapment.

Flying around thunderstorms may often be necessary to effectively use an airplane in the summertime. Just keep on top of one of the fastest changing situations in weather, and always maintain an "out" so you can land to sit out a big line of cells, rather than tackle them in the air.

Chapter 19

Squall Line Encounter

In all of nature's weather arsenal, there is perhaps no more awesome sight than the approach of a rapidly moving line of thunderstorms. The clear, slightly-hazy sky will contain a few distant thunderheads by midafternoon, easily dismissed as isolated air mass storms that will live out their lives in their present location and be of no great hindrance to cross-country flying. Should there be a strong weather system moving into the region, however, these distant storms may draw closer together and intensify, developing as a squall line ahead of the cold front.

You will usually be warned of this possibility if you secure a weather briefing from a Flight Service Station. Even if the weather check is skipped, however, or if the FSS briefing is running a little behind the actual situation, it takes no great amount of weather wisdom to tell what's going to happen. A portion of the sky that has grown visibly darker in the past hour or so must have something pretty potent behind it, and no one can look up at the towering side of a rapidly building cumulus without feeling rather insignificant and small.

Watching the Giants Approach

As experienced from the ground, an expectant hush falls as the line approaches. Not a leaf stirs. The hot, muggy air leaves the wind sock hanging limp. The darkening mass of water-filled storm cloud stretches to 40,000 feet or more, blocking out the sun's light as it nears. A few puffs of stratocumulus may float past, torn loose from the front of the storm line like bits of cotton candy. The viewer hears an artillery-like rumble of thunder and sees abundant cloud-to-ground lightning. Dust swirls up from open fields well in advance of the rain, the first gusts of the storm hitting the ground like the bow wave of a giant ocean liner. A cold upper-atmosphere wind strikes suddenly, spinning the wind sock around from its listless parked position with 40-knot gusts.

Minutes later, a roll of low stratus cloud sweeps by a few hundred feet overhead, condensation caused by the sudden introduction of cold air to the warm, moisture-laden air at ground level. As pilots frantically run to check their tiedowns and control locks, the rain hits, first with large, pellet-size drops, then blowing in with hurricane-like sheets as the storm intensifies. Wind gusts of 60 knots or more are commonplace.

Fortunately, the tempest's fury is short-lived; thunderstorm lines are usually no more than 20 to 40 miles wide, and within 30 minutes the rain will slacken and the winds subside as the storm moves on, leaving overturned airplanes and sodden turf in its wake. While it's possible for tornados to be lurking within these fast-moving lines, the twisters rarely are seen and most damage reports actually originate with the strong straight winds. Heavy hail can occur in localized areas, and light hail will be found in the clear air outside the rainshafts, falling from the overhanging anvil downwind from the storm. Severe wind shear can be encountered near the ground as an aircraft climbs or descends through one layer of moving air into another.

As Seen from the Air

Impressive as the storm appears from the ground, it is even more awesome when seen at close range in the air. Flying through turbulent but sunny skies, the pilot awakens to the fact that his windshield is growing dark. A glance upward through the haze reveals giant towers of cumulus ahead, and the wise pilot will check for a suitable landing spot close by. Pressing on, as many will, discloses the lightning-filled maw of the squall line. Heavy rain fills the void from the low cloud base to the ground, and the cloud stretches up to infinity. The air may be relatively smooth until within a few miles of the actual storm cloud, but when the first gust of the storm line is felt, there will seldom be further need to convince the pilot to go elsewhere.

Thunderstorm turbulence is of a different quality than that experienced in normal flatland thermals, more on the order of a strong mountain wave. The airplane is no longer capable of being precisely controlled, and the pilot feels as if he were in the grip of a giant, malevolent hand that is tossing the airplane up and down like a toy. These are the giant swells of the air, breaking into heavy seas

Fig. 19-1. A squall line advances across the countryside, bringing a wall of water and intense lightning. The low cloud warns of cold air pushed ahead of the line, and the car headlights on the highway tell of poor visibility even for driving. The winds went from calm to 40 knots-plus a few minutes after this picture was taken.

where opposing currents meet. The airplane is simply carried away, rising smoothly with the VSI needle pegged at 2000 fpm or dropped wrenching with the seat belt cutting into one's lap. The pilot's best course is to turn tail and run at the first contact with a thunderstorm's vertical currents, before penetrating any heavy rain that will block a clear view of retreat. If this option has already passed and the aircraft is committed to a penetration of the storm line, a power reduction should be made to slow the airplane to maneuvering speed and concentration applied to maintaining a constant heading that will hopefully lead one out of the storm after a few terror-filled minutes. Thunderstorms are like alcoholism: Abstinence is the only sure cure.

Close Encounter of the Worst Kind

My most memorable brush with a fast-moving thunderstorm line came not on a cross-country flight but at a prosaic airport picnic, one of those informal affairs where everybody brings a little something and much good fellowship is exchanged. There being no aerobatic aces on hand, I was enjoined to add a little color to the procedings by flying a few maneuvers in a Cessna 150 for the crowd. Nothing illegal, to be sure, just the usual training stuff that might be demonstrated in a commercial pilot program—60° steep turns, an accelerated stall, and a two-turn spin, with a few lazy eights and some chandelles thrown in to gain height for the finale, a deadstick landing with a rollout calculated to end in front of the hangar. Strictly showoff stuff, heavy on the grandstanding and short on precision—or, in this case, common sense.

As I taxied out, I realized that the line which was building in the northwest for the past hour or so had grown closer and I wondered at the wisdom of putting on my act. ("Shucks, it'll only take ten minutes; surely the rain will hold off that long.") I made a max-performance V_x climbout with all the pizzaz a 150 is capable of developing, and climbed toward the storm line to check it out. ("If it's closer and meaner than I think it is, I'll be in a position to run for the barn.") I could see no nearby rain shafts, the dark cloud base was well above me at 3000 feet AGL, and launched into my few minutes of tomfoolery for the benefit of those watching below. I noticed a strong tendency to drift away from the storm. This stiff horizontal flow should have warned me that things were moving fast.

As soon as my brief sequence was finished, I chopped the mixture back and pulled up to stop the prop, noticing an approaching roll of gray cumulus. The storm was coming fast; I needed to be on the ground *now* and it would take five minutes to execute the deadstick approach. I checked my altitude and was shocked to find it *increasing* rather than decreasing! I pushed over instinctively, a reflex action to avoid the threatening wall of dark cloud at my elbow; I was indicating well over 100 mph and the VSI showed a 500-fpm climb with the prop stopped. There was no turbulence, just a smooth, elevator-like upward pull. The situation was out of control; I could see the cloud base nearing rapidly. I was about to go IMC with inoperative gyros, sucked up by a huge vacuum cleaner.

To heck with the airshow! I turned to a right angle from the storm line's axis and ran away from the airport, heading for the clear air at V_a speed, trying not to exceed maneuvering speed in case I hit rough air that could overstress the airplane. I cranked the engine back to life to regain suction power for the gyros and to get a little extra drag from the windmilling prop. At the same time, I lowered 40° of flaps for maximum drag. Lowering the flaps reduced the protection offered by maneuvering speed, but I was wanting out of this and would try anything to increase my sink rate. After several long, anxious seconds of running from the storm the VSI dropped below zero into the "down" half of the dial, and I ran the flaps up and began to breathe a little easier.

Any Port in a Storm

It was time to review the situation. There was no weather ahead; an alternate airport lay some 25 miles away. On the other hand, the home field was only a few miles behind me. A glance over my shoulder showed that the automatic lighting system had turned itself on because of the darkness overhead, but there was no rain and I could see under the storm for 10 miles or more. I decided there was time enough to make one try at the runway. I expected heavy winds at the surface, and, if I had to abandon my landing attempt, I could head for the alternate. I bored toward the runway with cruise power, making good a groundspeed of perhaps 60 mph. The final approach was flown at 90 mph with flaps up, to make any sort of headway, and I only reduced power as the threshold neared. Fortunately, the wind was directly down the runway, because the sock was standing straight out and whipping to and fro, a sign of 35 knots plus. The touchdown was as soft as a thistledown due to the ultra-slow groundspeed, and several pilots wingwalked me into the lee of a hangar to receive the welcome due a victorious warrier returning from battle. Minutes later the wind was 90° to the runway with heavy rain.

Instead, I should have received the reward of a bonehead, with a severe flogging for endangering both an airplane and my own skin. Mistake number one was taking off in the face of oncoming weather simply due to the press of "business," plus continued adherence to the planned activity until it nearly became too late. Only the god who looked after fools gave me a dry cloud base and winds aligned with the runway just long enough to make it home. It would have served me right to have spent the night sleeping in the airplane at an alternate field, fighting mosquitos in the heat.

Chapter 20

Managing Heat Stress

When the heat's on, it brings a host of problems for the summertime aviator. If you live in a part of the country where the midday temperatures crowd the century mark, or if you visit such areas, be ready to deal with the temperature's trials.

As you no doubt know, airplanes in general, and low-wing airplanes in particular, get beastly hot inside the cabin when sitting out in the sun. With the doors and windows tightly shut, it can get well over 130 degrees inside, enough to warp plastic plotters and make a pilot's thinking processes less than sharp.

So do what you can to cool things down inside. Park in the shade if at all possible, open the doors and windows for ventilation while doing the preflight inspection, and keep the time on the ground to an absolute minimum. Grass parking areas tend to be a little cooler than the sun-baked expanses of concrete or asphalt. Invest in a sunscreen of space-blanket material to cover your windows when parked, or fabricate something similar or your own.

Taking Care of the Engine

Don't forget about the torrid conditions under the cowling, where the engine lives. A modern air-cooled powerplant was designed to be operated in flight, where the cooling air can blast around the fins and carry the heat out of the cowling. As the power output demanded from engines has been steadily increased through the years, the cowling and baffling have been refined for the utlimate reduction in drag to best utilize this extra power—all of which leaves an engine that can't be operated for prolonged periods on the ground, or in high-angle climbs, without overheating.

Therefore, be as easy as possible on your engine; don't warm it up too long, just enough to stabilize the oil pressure before taxiing.

By the time you reach the end of the runway and complete a runup in 100° weather, it'll be ready to go. Face into the wind if parking for any length of time, double-check that the cowl flaps are open, if you have them, and monitor the temperature gauges. The cylinder head temperature will react faster than oil temperature, but remember the instruments are only measuring the health of the engine at one specific point, so there's no guarantee that another area of the engine isn't already overheating by the time a redline is indicated.

Preventive Maintenance

Before summer really arrives, take the cowling off and put mama's vacuum cleaner to work sucking out the leftover bird nests from between the cylinder fins and baffles. This accumulation can cause hot spots and maybe a top overhaul. The seasonal oil change would be a logical time to clean out the engine compartment, as well as to check for loose or damaged baffle plates.

The engine's oil level should be kept topped off without over-filling, since this is the major heat-exchanging medium within an air-cooled engine. If the oil is allowed to get a few quarts low, it just isn't going to carry away as much heat as it passes around the engine.

Hot weather also plays havoc with radio gear. It's a good idea to check all the cooling provisions—such as vent openings, fans, and blast tubes—that keep the black boxes operating at their best. Don't run every radio in the house unnecessarily while on the ground unless your cooling setup is able to handle it. It's true that the transistorized units don't generate as much heat as the old tube-type sets, but they are also much less tolerant of high temperatures; consequently they must be protected from potential heat stroke.

Hot Starts

Getting the engine restarted after a fast fuel stop can often be a trial, especially for fuel-injected airplanes. Everyone is hot and miserable, anxious to be back upstairs in the cool, while the pilot cranks fruitlessly. The problem—and hence the solution—varies from aircraft to aircraft. It can be vapor lock, the particular plague of fuel-injection; a fuel line gets warm enough under the confines of the cowling to cause a vapor bubble to form and block fuel flow. The answer is to force the vapor through the lines with positive fuel pressure from the boost pump, or perhaps to start the engine on primer if available. The danger in this is over-priming, perhaps accumulating excess fuel in the induction system where it can catch fire as the engine starts. Use the boost pump only until fuel pressure is steady, then shut it off to attempt a start. Don't use the hand primer without cranking, and if you do get a stack fire, keep cranking to suck the flames into the engine, where they can do no harm.

The opposite extreme is flooding the engine with excessive fuel so that it fires only fitfully with puffs of black smoke. Just pull the mixture into idle-cutoff and crank once more, pushing the mixture back into full-rich when the engine comes to life; opening the throttle speeds the process. Some engines flood easily when hot; others won't start without plenty of fuel. It's best to try a lean start first, then add fuel later if that doesn't work. Best of all, just follow the instructions in the Pilot's Operating Handbook; the people who built the airplane knew best.

Sagging Performance

Summer brings a compromise in overall aircraft performance; the old bird lifted off readily with a full load in the winter, but she's a different airplane when the mercury soars. The low density of the hot, humid air saps power from the engine, and also hampers the wing's ability to produce lift, adding up to our old friend, density altitude trouble. So what if the field elevation is only 3500 feet? Crank the temperature up to 100°, maybe more just above the surface of the runway, and it becomes 7000 feet for all the airplane knows. Pad those figures in the owner's manual plenty, and don't think your troubles are over just because you made it into the air. The rate of climb is going to be less than outstanding, perhaps only a couple hundred feet per minute at full bore, and strong downdrafts will be more than you can outclimb despite your best efforts. A few minutes of fighting your way uphill at V_y speed and your engine will be hollering for mercy as the oil temp nears the redline.

The moral of the story is: *Don't fight the temperature, learn to live with it.* Fly early and late, avoiding the full heat of the day whenever possible. Don't load up your airplane to the limit; leave a seat empty instead. Climb at higher speeds to keep the engine cool, and level off momentarily if the temperature gauges leave the green. Don't yank the nose up to fight a downdraft, just keep going and fly out of it; your flight path may be erratic, but the engine will stay cooler.

The usual summer flight plan is to climb until you find smooth air, then level off at the next available cruising altitude. This often puts you on top of the scattered cumulus puffs that mark the rising thermals. Make sure you don't get pushed higher and higher by the building of baby thunderstorms until you are suddenly in the middle of one that is outclimbing you. Better get back down below if the tops threaten to engulf you. The rough ride at lower altitudes can generally be avoided by flying early in the day.

Don't overlook the effects of summer on you, the pilot. Heat and humidity are tiring stresses, and a fever is a fever, whether it comes from an illness or an overheated cockpit. Keep your body full of liquids and take a rest break now and again, letting your copilot take a turn at the wheel. Use a set of lightweight headphones so you won't irritate the passengers by battling the shrieking ventilators with a loud loudspeaker. These are little things, but accidents are often the result of little things that added up. When you keep your cool the flight just seems to go better.

Summer is a great time to fly. Enjoy the fair skies and long daylight hours, but respect the special terms of this hot-weather season.

Chapter 21

The Hazy Days of Summer

Low visibility haze conditions are increasingly becoming a fact of life for cross-country pilots, especially during the warm weather months. Flying in the semi-VFR whiteout of severe haze can be an unnerving experience for low-time pilots, and a nuisance even for experienced ones. There are few tasks more difficult than keeping one's aircraft straight and level when the only ground reference is straight below. Taken to extremes, this difficulty winds up under the accident classification "attempted continued VFR flight into IFR weather conditions."

What's Haze, Anyway?

Haze is a restriction to visibility with no measurable cloud present. It differs from fog in that a fog layer can be seen and measured; the cloud is at the surface or slightly above it, with a relatively low top. Haze, on the other hand, is not a visible cloud. It can be tenuous and difficult to measure, and it often extends to 10,000 feet above the surface. It can be a local condition caused by heavy pollution and moist air being "capped" over a city by a temperature inversion, or it can be a widespread air mass condition, when moist air stagnates instead of following the general west-to-east movement across the continent. Wooded hills are often wrapped in the blue haze of warm moist air restricted in its movement by ridges and valleys.

Coping Inflight

It is by no means simple to avoid flying in marginal-VFR haze. The ground visibility can be quite acceptable, with perhaps five miles reported, while the inflight visibility can be a mile or less, particularly near the condensation level where small puffs of cumulus are attempting to form. You can depart with every assurance that the enroute weather is good VFR, and find yourself in practically IFR conditions. It behooves every pilot to be ready to cope with such an eventuality.

If you are instrument-rated and prepared to file IFR if the need arises, you will probably opt for flying VFR on top of the haze, which can require a cruise altitude of 8,500 to 12,500 feet. This will place you in clear air, where you can see approaching traffic and distant weather in unlimited visibility. This is also a tempting choice for the VFR pilot, but one that should be used with discretion. Flight above a haze layer can be the same as flying over a cloud layer; the top may not be horizontal, giving you the "leans" due to a false horizon, and to avoid getting lost you should stick to the airways or routes you know to have adequate VOR reception. Since you must descend VFR, be alert for a ceiling developing below your flight level.

On short flights it may be impractical to climb above the haze, and it will be necessary to fly down in the soup with everyone else. IFR pilots will feel more comfortable with a clearance, but they should be aware that VFR traffic is quite legally boring around in the haze with them, and they should keep a sharp lookout. If you are flying a fast airplane in a busy traffic area IFR, with no autopilot, press a front-seat passenger into service to help keep watch.

The VFR pilot must respect his limitations in haze, and those of his equipment. It is possible to fly in somewhat worse conditions with an aritificial horizon and gyro compass than with a basic 1946 instrument panel, but you shouldn't continue indefinitely with less than three miles of visibility, or in *any* case with one mile or less. There are too many unmarked towers out there, and the faster the airplane, the less time you will have for avoidance.

Navigation Chores

Pilotage navigation will be difficult at best, as the landmarks loom up and disappear before you have time to check them fully on the chart. It is not wise to draw a line across the countryside and expect to follow it as you might in clear weather. Low-level winds aloft reports being what they are, you can easily drift off course by five miles in short order, and that's enough to leave you disoriented in three-mile haze. It is far better to use an alternate route, such as a VOR airway or other usable radial. One of the best methods is to swallow your pride and lock onto a good highway, river, or railroad track, following it to your destination. By doing so, you will know part of your location at all times, by having a line of position, and it will be simpler to identify each town or checkpoint as it comes down the road. Airports are generally located along these lines of surface transportation, so you can easily make that 180° turn and follow the road back to a safe haven if it gets too bad.

When forced to follow such an impromptu course line as a road, make note of the time over various points along the way, writing the minutes figure right on the chart beside the point. Should you become disoriented later, you will at least have a basis for knowing your last position and the time over it.

The time of day naturally has much to do with the inflight visibility in haze. An early morning eastbound trip, or an evening westbound flight, can reduce seven miles of reported surface visibility to less than a mile at altitude. The light rays are scattered and diffused by the haze to create an almost total whiteout when looking into the sun. Try a lower altitude in such cases to bring more of the ground into view for attitude reference. Should you be flying with the sun at your back, remember that approaching traffic will be blinded by the up-sun viewing angle, and may not spot you until dangerously close.

VFR in IFR Conditions

The greatest challenge to flying VFR in haze is the continual switching from visual to instrument references and back again. You will be looking at the ground below, comparing it to the chart, and then, upon glancing back at the panel you will notice that your heading has changed 10 or 20 degrees, or that the altitude has slipped up or down a bit. You make a correction, probably by using the artificial horizon and other instruments, then go back to looking at the milk-bottle void outside, once again drifting away from straight and level flight. Learn to relax at the controls while looking outside, flying "loose" just as you would in good VFR conditions. Panic and fighting the controls will not help your situation.

Fortunately, the country is fairly replete with VOR stations, and you can often keep a running crosscheck of your progress by dialing a "from" reading from two stations, since you may need to confirm your exact position when landmarks slip by without ample time to check them out. Don't be afraid to get a DF steer from a tower or FSS that advertises this service in its data block. Being too proud to admit you're not sure of your position has taken many a pilot past the point of no return.

Other Weather Hazards

Be alert for an embedded thunderstorm lurking in the haze like a shark in the surf. If the haze suddenly darkens ahead, take notice; a boomer is probably casting its shadow on the top of the haze layer. If the cloud is only a good healthy building cumulus, with plenty of clear space underneath, lighter skies will reappear beyond the cloud base. But a spatter of rain on the windshield should mean a 180 for the VFR pilot, back to the last airport. Dodging embedded cells is a game for those equipped with airborne radar or stormscope devices, and even then it's pretty exciting.

Should you be running into scud, losing sight of the ground occasionally, don't press your luck. Stay below the clouds, even though you have reports of excellent weather ahead, if they keep lowering as the haze thickens; don't gamble on sneaking through with only a few hundred feet of altitude and no visibility. You are probably trying to bust through a stationary front, and the good weather reports are from the cold air sector beyond the down-to-the-ground frontal zone. Many good pilots have died trying to make it those last few miles, so don't add your name to the list by flying into a hillside or tower.

The term *air stagnation* has become all too familiar as mankind continues to foul its own nest and nature occasionally pours a strong temperature inversion into the witches' cauldron. Pilots will find themselves forced to fly in haze or not make use of their airplanes at all, so you had best learn to cope with it, within your limitations.

Chapter 22

Fog, the Insidious Enemy

Fog is one of aviation's undefeated evil triumvirate, its partners being thunderstorms and icing. While fog may not bring airplanes swiftly to earth when first encountered, its ability to eventually halt all operations is certain. To cope with fog, there are a few Category II instrument approaches around—and an equally few pilots approved to use them. However, the CAT II approach only permits landings down to a visibility of roughly one-quarter mile and a decision height of 100 feet, so the final transition to the ground must still be made with visual reference to the runway unless one wishes to trust the triple computers of an autoland system.

There are times when the fog thickens even below instrument landing minimums. Grounded, despite all our ratings and equipment, we pace the floors of airport lounges and spend hours on the phone reshuffling plans, cursing our fate, and wondering when the weather service people will learn to cast their chicken bones properly so we can get an accurate forecast. It's important to understand the nature of any enemy if you intend to challenge him successfully. Fog is an enemy, to be sure.

Forecasting fog with any degree of precision is guesswork. It's easy for a prognosticator to foresee the chance of fog occurring, but that doesn't mean it will necessarily happen. A degree or two of temperature can make all the difference in the world. As can a few knots of wind or a change in the amount of moisture in the air. Fog can be so localized that forecasting from any distance is impossible. You must be your own forecaster, or suffer the consequences of a useless forecast.

When Will Fog Appear?

Fog is basically a cloud whose base is at the surface, one

obscuring the sky rather than forming a ceiling overhead. A condition reported as haze is simply fog of a different degree, when saturation of the air is not complete. When fog is at the surface, a typical observed ceiling will be reported as "100 obscured," meaning that the ceilometer penetrates 100 feet into the cloud, not that the base is 100 feet above the surface as with a normal ceiling report. Looking forward through the windshield from an altitude of 100 feet requires perhaps five times as much distance to see the runway as looking straight down; obviously, you aren't going to see anything but fog when attempting to land. A report of a partial obscuration may tempt you to try to get in, but have an alternate handy because "partial" can become "total" on the very next ATIS.

The thickness of a fog layer greatly affects your chances of getting into—or out of—a particular airport. While fog typically burns off after sunup at the rate of about 100 feet per hour, a cirrus layer holding back the sun's warming rays can keep it from breaking open at all, and added moisture from an overrunning layer of air will refuel the fog generator. Still, just being able to take a look at the actual sky condition above the fog can make all the difference.

IFR Launch Decisions

There probably isn't an instrument-rated pilot in the world who

Fig. 22-1. The airport is nearly IFR, with visibility of 1½ miles in light fog. This is no time to attempt VFR flight; wait for an improving trend.

can resist a glimpse of clear blue sky through a break in a fog layer, even if the runway visual range is only 1200 feet. That revealing hole is all he needed to load up and go, assuming there is an alternate field within reasonable range to handle contingencies after departure. The pilot knows there'll only be about one minute of actual instrument flying on each end of the trip. On the other hand, should the sky have that thick, dark, gray look characteristic of solid multi-layered weather, the trip will be much more challenging, requiring greater care in selecting alternates and balancing fuel reserves, particularly if the traffic flow is heavy enough to create enroute delays. A recent pilot report is worth more than all the guesses of the weather service.

Fog Formation

Whence cometh the fog, on its little cat feet? From condensation, my dears, only that and nothing more. Water vapor condenses into visible cloud when the air mass reaches saturation, and one need only add more water to an air mass of a given temperature, or reduce the temperature of an air mass with a given percentage of saturation, to trigger fog. No moisture, no fog; it's that simple. This explains why temperature and dewpoint can often sit perilously close to each other without fog appearing, or why fog can appear when the spread isn't razor-thin.

If the moisture is present already, nighttime cooling can reduce air temperatures to the condensation point, generating patchy radiation fog. A strong flow of warm, moist air over cold, frozen ground can create widespread zero-zero conditions as advection fog. A weak cold front can stall out against a warm air mass, fogging in the frontal boundary. Or a sea breeze can move cool offshore moisture tightly against a wall of steeply-rising terrain to sock in the coast. These are all examples of fog's origins.

Is fog strictly an instrument pilot's problem? Hardly, considering that clear air is normally only a few hundred feet away vertically, inviting the VFR pilot to fly over and take a look, or to depart in hopes of finding a hole. These sucker traps are deadly, and require cautious planning to avoid.

Our purpose here is to give you advice on how to cope with fog, rather than to provide a meteorology lesson, but it is important for you to understand the basics so you'll know when you can't win. There's no point in trying to get into an airport that's never going to get up to minimums, nor should you bother dragging your passengers out to the airport just to sit around the waiting room. Take all fog predictions with a barrel of salt, realizing that forecasters can't foresee every local aberration in terrain, wind speed, or upper cloud deck; remember, the weather is what it *is*, not what it's forecast to be.

Betting on Your Chances

When faced with a cheery forecast but a poor current sequence, assume the skeptical stance of a used-car prospect. Don't bet your life on any forecast until it starts to happen. You may be legal to launch without an alternate according to the forecast, but you'll wish you had one when the "clearing after seventeen-hundred local" doesn't materalize. A burnoff is possible only if certain conditions are met—no more moisture coming in, no higher clouds, no change in wind estimates. When the forecast doesn't start to come true by midmorning after a night of fog formation, throw it away; you can bet that an amended one will be coming out at the appointed time.

Another classic sucker job is the predawn departure under the stars, a trap that boxes in many VFR pilots. Anxious to get an early start, our hero dutifully checks his route while half-asleep, finds everything clear, and launches with his landing lights ablaze. There's a hint of trouble when condensation trails are seen wisping from the prop tips on takeoff. The sun peeps over the horizon an hour or so later, and mini-thermals start mixing the encapsulated pockets of moisture near the ground. Non-homogeneous streams of low-lying fog in the valleys start to climb up out of their beds, swallowing the plains, and suddenly there is a blanket of white everywhere. Hopefully, a few hilltop airports will remain open to receive visitors, or maybe the sun will work its magic before the fuel runs out. Meanwhile, one more pilot has received his education about fog.

The cure for fog is avoidance, just as with our other two assassins, thunderstorms and ice. Avoidance means adapting a forecast to your own location's conditions, asking a lot of questions of the natives if you're not at home, and tempering your boldness with an honest appraisal of your ability to fly. Lots of fuel and a wide-open VFR alternate—these are the tools we rely on to defeat the insidious enemy called fog.

Chapter 23

A Cold, Cold Start

It comes at the end of every autumn. It's that time of the year when the engine oil turns to Jell-O, frost coats the windshield, and last summer's battery loses its ability to spin the prop rapidly. Winter is back and the annual battle to start a reluctant machine is joined once more.

Getting the bird started is an elementary task in warm temperatures; jump pump the throttle once, twist the key, and you're off and running. But when the temperature drops below 40° F., the task is no longer so simple. Pilots of southern-based airplanes may find this out the hard way when they make an overnight cross-country into the northern states. There, 50-weight oil and tropical starting procedures just don't cut it. They will all too often wind up summoning aid to get the airplane started—unnecessarily at times. By taking a few minutes to think about cold-weather starting, you may save yourself embarrassment and a few bucks.

What's the Problem?

It's no mere accident that airplane engines are hard to start when cold. They are practically designed to be that way, with large per-cylinder displacement, heavy-viscosity lubricating oil, and a relatively crude updraft carburetor, further hampered by a battery smaller than that used by a garden tractor. Compared with automobile engines, it's a wonder the darned things start at all. Sometimes they just *won't* out of sheer cussedness—usually when a hurried departure is necessary to meet a schedule.

There are tricks of the trade, however. First, preheat the engine if at all possible; that's old advice, but it's still sound. Bringing the cylinder heads, oil pan, and induction system up to 50° or so ensures a prompt start, without washing the residual film of oil from the cylinder walls by heavy priming. The good folks in the northern border states know all about this and they can't believe that pilots in the middle layer of the country will actually attempt starts in near-zero weather without preheating.

Adding a Little Heat

Preheating apparatus need not be elaborate. If a small heat source is used, such as a heat lamp or a firepot, it will be necessary to drape a tent around the cowling to contain the heat. Take care to keep flammable materials a good distance away from the heat source, and stay nearby to watch over things during the warm-up. Electric dipstick heaters can be useful to thaw the stiff oil, and by turning the prop over you can pump warm oil through the engine, but you should be aware that many of the newer Lycoming oil-filler tubes are plastic, and consequently should not be subjected to heat. The fastest and most reliable heat is delivered by an oil-fired space heater, the kind that looks and sounds like a small jet engine, either blowing its heat through flexible ducts or simply aimed into the cowl openings from the back of a pickup truck. Fifteen minutes of the dragon's breath and ol' Betsy will start at the touch of a key.

Fig. 23-1. A jury-rigged pre-heating setup, usable with electricity near the airplane. The space heater must be kept far enough away from the cowling to avoid scorching paint, and equal time is given to both cowl openings. The windshield requires deicing also.

Nearly all preheating requires electricity, and that may be the limiting factor in your own situation. The tiedown or hangar may be far away from an electrical outlet, and the footing may be too slippery to allow walking the airplane to the source of power. If there is no other choice, a cold start may be attempted, but it is not only hard on the equipment, the outcome is far less sure. Down to about 20° F a cold start is generally possible, given some experience with the airplane's characteristics. Below that figure, chances are reduced to 50/50 at 10°, and about nil at 0° F. There it will take luck, skill, and several degrees of incantations to bring the bird to life.

Most of our starting-procedure tips are directed toward carburetor-equipped engines. Fuel-injected airplanes have an easier time of it but are still hampered by the poor performance of the battery and the thick oil. The advantage of fuel injection stems from the availability of positive fuel flow directly to the cylinders; carburetor-equipped airplanes will have priming systems that can deliver fuel to the intake manifold while cranking, but it often takes more hands than you've got to prime, crank, and work the throttle. All cylinders are not primed evenly, if they are even primed at all; many airplanes have systems that only prime one or two cylinders.

Giving It a Try

Begin by verifying that the ignition switch is turned off and by expending a little of your own muscle, turning the propeller through by hand to limber up the oil so the battery won't have to do it. Then prime the engine several strokes, leaving the primer pulled out, and immediately turn the propeller over by hand about four compression strokes to load the cylinders with fuel with the throttle wide open. Jump into the saddle, pull the throttle back, and hit the starter before the primer fuel evaporates. Make sure all lights and other electrical items are off so every available amp is directed to the starter motor.

If the engine fires, keep it running by using the primer on the carburetor's accelerator pump, by rapidly pumping the throttle through the first half of its travel. Avoid pumping the throttle with fuel-injected engines, however, because it has no effect other than to confuse the fuel-metering mechanism. Just hit the boost pump to keep a fuel-injected engine going if it tries to die.

If at First You Don't Succeed

If you don't meet with success immediately, don't keep cranking, expecting a miracle. If there's no response after a dozen revolutions, save the battery and try something different. Look under the cowling for dripping fuel, which is a sign of excessive priming and throttle pumping. This causes the gasoline to drain back down through the intake pipes and out the carburetor body, pooling under the cowling. As a fire hazard, this is one of the many undesirable features of a cold start. It pays to have a fire extinguisher handy in case of backfire through the intake pipes ignites the pooled gasoline. Don't panic if a fire is detected in the carburetor, just continue cranking the engine to draw the flames into the cylinders where they can do no harm. Move the airplane away from spilled gasoline, if possible, or wait for it to evaporate.

When dripping fuel is seen do not prime further but open the throttle fully and crank the engine to clear the flooded mixture. Be ready to bring the throttle back if the engine starts (to prevent high rpm, which can cause extra-high oil pressure against the bearing seals). Most likely there will be no start, and it is best to discontinue cranking after a few revolutions. The engine can also be cleared by opening the throttle and turning the prop by hand with the switch off to save the battery. Then close the throttle and begin all over again.

If no dripping primer fuel is seen, add a few more priming strokes and engage the starter once more. It helps to have the primer charged and ready for action in case it's needed to keep the engine running, but push the primer knob in slowly so the engine won't flood. Fitful attempts to run are usually a sign of flooding, while no firing at all is more common and an indication of insufficient fuel. Immediate starting followed by silence can be taken to mean primer fuel was burned but the induction system fuel was not reaching the cylinders in time; try again, adding more priming fuel.

Taking Care of the Engine

By all means, keep the engine running after it starts; if moisture is present in the air, a few seconds of firing followed by a shutdown will invite condensation in the form of frost on the spark plug electrodes and there can usually be no further ignition until the plugs are removed and dried or the engine is heated. Watch the tach carefully for the first 60 seconds and pump the throttle or hit the boost pump if it falters.

Battery life is usually measured in seconds during winter starts, particularly if the battery has several seasons on it. Jumper starts are often necessary and can provide the extra amps sorely needed by the starter motor. Just watch your polarity when hooking up to avoid lunching the alternator, and make sure all avionics are off to keep them safe from odd voltages coming through the system. Avoid having extra people around during jump-start operations so a preoccupied onlooker won't walk into a prop while helping with cables or whatever. If you have one of the newer airplanes with a 24-volt battery, forget about jump-starting from your car; you'll have to hunt an FBO with a battery cart.

Fuel vaporization is difficult with high-density cold air, even after the engine is running; warming up with the carburetor heat on may be advisable to help the engine accelerate when throttle is applied. In extreme cold, this may actually induce carb ice by warming the carburetor into the ice-prone range, but such occurrences seem to be rare. Keep some power on during flight to maintain heat in the engine and avoid shock-cooling the cylinder heads by rapid heating and cooling, which can cause cracked cylinders. Handle the throttle gingerly, taking two seconds to reach full travel to avoid stalling the engine.

Take advantage of any winterization equipment provided, such as baffles for the cowl openings, insulation for the oil tank and breather pipe, and bypass routing for the oil radiator. These items, like preheating, will add hours of life to your engine; each cold start probably costs the equivalent of two or three hours of wear, so you should avoid needless starts and short trips. If you *must* go when the mercury is near the bottom of the tube, give it your best and perhaps you'll get away with it.

Chapter 24

Ice: the Plane Chiller

Ice! The very word itself seems to have a chilling effect, as when shouted by a bowsprit lookout on a sailing schooner groping its way through a fog-shrouded North Atlantic. Soon after airmen first began trying to fly on through the winter months, they ran afoul of icing's insidious effect on airplanes, and the battle between the airman and the elements has raged ever since.

Learning conditions that foster ice formation, and the options available to cope with it, is time well spent for all winter-flying pilots. For most of the lighter segments of aviation, the best remedy will be avoidance. Don't go where the ice is, and leave it where you find it. When you play the game of how-much-will-it carry, particularly in a minimally equipped airplane, you're playing with fire, not just ice, and every winter several pilots get burned.

These words are not just for the cloud-fliers; a note of caution is also in order about VFR icing. Oh, yes, ice can mess up your VFR flying in several ways. No doubt we were all introduced to the carburetor heat control early in our careers; some of us may never have had cause to use it in anger, yet Ol' Man Carb Ice is out there, waiting, along with another VFR icetrap, freezing drizzle.

Carb Ice

Remember, aircraft carburetors are, for the most part, updraft installations, wherein the carburetor hangs below the engine in relatively cold air. When a liquid expands into a gaseous state, such as when fuel is vaporized in the carburetor, it quite naturally gets cool, just as you cool off by evaporating perspiration from your body. Thus, in the absence of rising warm air from a hot engine block, temperatures in the aircraft carburetor throat can drop below 32° Fahrenheit in an ambient temperature of 50° or more, and if moisture is present in the air, ice will form on such projections as the throttle valve. This has a choking effect due to the restriction of air volume but not fuel flow, and it causes the engine to lose power due to the excessively rich mixture. The condition is terminal in extreme cases, and if you wait until the engine's fire has gone out you will no longer have a source of heat to deice the carburetor. Early detection and prevention is the answer.

At the onset of carb ice, a slight power loss is noticed—a drop in rpm if flying a fixed-pitch propeller, or a loss of manifold pressure in a complex airplane. Thinking the throttle has crept back, the pilot will nudge the power back up. Soon, power will be back down again. If he doesn't get the message, he'll shortly wind up at full throttle with power still dropping off. For warning, check the prevailing conditions—look at the outside air temperature. If the temp is down in the Fahrenheit 40s or less, and there's any moisture around, you've certainly got carb ice. Moisture can be present in the clear air just below a cloud layer, in hazy but legal VFR conditions after fog dissipates, or downwind from large bodies of open water. Naturally, precipitation such as light rain or moist snow can do an excellent job of putting ice in your carburetor.

For fast, fast, fast relief, pull the carb heat knob full on, and leave it there despite the unnerving consequences. A badly iced-up engine may quit running briefly, bucking and snorting as the melted ice passes through its system. If you keep the faith, power will suddenly come back with a rush, and all your excess throttle will make its presence felt. You may, after clearing the carburetor throat, have to adjust the mixture for smooth operation, due to the lower density of the hot air, but leave the heat on regardless. A carburetor temperature gauge or ice detector is a nice insurance policy, if you have a spot on the panel for one.

There is a type of induction icing that can also plague non-carbureted airplanes in the form of air filters blocked with moist snow. Alternate air intake sources should be restore power if you encounter this problem with your fuel-injected engine.

VFR Airframe Ice

Ice on the windshield can readily shake up a supposedly VFR pilot. If you don't have a good defroster on your airplane, fly only in the clearest winter air. If you do have one, make sure you're familiar with its operation before winter sets in. If you should get into icing conditions, you at least want to be able to see to get back on the ground. Shutting off the cabin heat outlets will direct extra hot air to the windshield in some airplanes.

The VFR pilot can pick up a rapid glazing of clear ice in freezing rain conditions, despite relatively good visibility. The light rain showers look normal enough, inviting a direct flight through them, but if the outside air temperature is below freezing, watch out! The drops hit with more than the usual solidity, and within seconds your leading edges are painted a new shade of white. You've just had VFR ice, clear of clouds. Avoid any further showers and, if conditions are widespread, land at the first available aerodrome.

Ice and the Instrument Pilot

Instrument pilots, of course, know the patent remedy for freezing rain. Since it is falling from a warm layer of air overlying the cold air in which you're flying, you go up into the warm layer to get relief. Do not do so blindly, however, expecting no further trouble. Keep fuel and alternatives available in case you penetrate the upward slope of the cold air mass again, or if you run out of climb ability before reaching the warm air.

Flying in clouds at temperatures below freezing would seem to be a perfect setup for icing. However, IFR pilots learn that ice is difficult to forecast accurately, as they make flights unscathed when expecting to find trouble and pick up ice on other flights when no mention of it was made in the forecasts. Ice can be a very localized phenomenon, and the freezing level is not always level, often having ups and downs that cause you to run in and out of ice formation. In general, unstable air masses with vertical air movement will make ice formation difficult to predict. Even pilot reports may not be reliable, as one aircraft gets only frost and another reports moderate to heavy ice.

In any event, ice accumulation is your signal to take action. Rather than passively watching it build, hoping you'll get there before it gets too heavy, make some plans. Check weather reports for airports with above-freezing surface temperatures, in case you need to divert, and warn ATC you've got some ice and may want to change altitude. If ice continues to accumulate, *do* something. Request another altitude—either higher, hoping to get on top of the clouds or between layers, or lower if the surface temps are well above freezing. Don't forget you can always turn around and go back to where the ice wasn't forming—*you're* flying the airplane, you know, it's not being pulled to the destination on rails.

Even with anti-icing gear on your airplane, make contingency plans when you first hit ice. Light aircraft boots and prop deicers are

Fig. 24-1. Alcohol anti-icing, as installed on this Baron, can be used to prevent ice from sticking to the blades; channels in the rubber boots at the blade's cuff stream the fluid out along the metal blade. At best, any lightplane ice protection merely buys additional time to escape.

a compromise in weight versus capability, and it is unwise to think in terms of being able to handle any weather you come across. Anti-icing equipment is for buying time, allowing you more options to extricate yourself from the icy trap. Keep the wings and props waxed or siliconed if you will, but remember the Arab adage: "Trust in Allah but tie your camel."

Should you be forced to land with an accumulation of ice on the airplane, beware the increase in stall speed and drag caused by the weight and uneven surface of the ice. Tack on several extra knots and carry additional power for the approach, but not to the point of coming in too hot to land on the available runway.

Some of the best flying of the year comes in the winter, when the air is smooth and the density altitude is low. Ice is just a fact of life we must accept along with winter's benefits. Understand it and take action when you encounter it, don't wait until all your escape routes are closed.

Chapter 25

Flying Snow

When winter spreads its annual blanket of white over much of the U.S., pilots who fly after snowstorms are often faced with a clear sky but an uncleared runway. Operators of north country airfields usually make every effort to plow the runways and ramps as soon as possible, because another layer may come with the next weather system and the snow would soon be too deep to handle. In the lower tiers of snow states, however, where the white stuff comes less often, smaller airfields may be dependent on hard-pressed road and street crews to clear the city's runways. The airport can remain unplowed for days while the trucks fight to keep the roads open. Right or wrong, that's the way it happens, and the wise pilot always calls ahead to check the condition of the field he intends to use after a snowstorm.

Checking It Out from the Ground

Assuming you've encountered a thoroughly snowed-upon airport, how would you cope with it? If you are on the ground, the obvious first step would be to survey the depth of the snow cover, either on foot or from a suitable vehicle. Using a car with street tires is asking for a long, cold walk when you get struck in a drift at the far end of the runway, so a four-wheel drive vehicle, tractor, or snowmobile would be best. In addition to reconnaissance, the vehicle's tires or treads will leave tracks useful for reference during takeoff and landing on fresh snow.

How much snow is *too* much? As with grass, mud, or sand, it depends on the airplane involved. A two-place airplane with fat tires can negotiate four or perhaps even six inches of loose snow, while some four-placers might be stopped by three inches. Larger aircraft sometimes can make up for a lack of flotation with brute horsepower,

115

but it's not wise to make a practice of taxiing with nearly full power. Tightly cowled engines can become overheated due to lack of adequate airflow without the pilot's knowledge, especially when headed downwind.

Packed, dense snow on a hard runway presents far less challenge than loose, drifted snow, such as might be found on a turf runway. Fortunately, airports are generally built in the open countryside where the wind blows freely, and you may find your problem is getting through the drifts around the hangar, with the runway itself having accumulated only an inch of hard snow. Asphalt runways melt snow nicely once the sun gets through the white reflective layer of snow; the black absorbs heat rays and gains enough warmth to thaw even at sub-freezing temperatures.

Assessing the Situation from the Air

If you are airborne when you encounter a snowy runway, you are obviously in a much poorer position to make a decision about using the strip. Unicom can help, but not every airport has radio equipment, and Flight Service only knows about the status of the airports whose operators choose to call in. If you see a large "X" marking the center of the airport or at runway ends, take the hint and go elsewhere; the field or runway is officially closed.

Fig. 25-1. This large metropolitan airport is open, with all runways plowed, but some ramps were still ice-covered. Surburban fields may not be so lucky, however.

Lacking any information about the field, you can try dragging it at an altitude of 50 feet or so to look for clues to the snow depth. Runway light fixtures, markers, fence posts, parked airplanes, and so forth can help gauge the accumulation, but these should be backed up by watching for tire tracks left by other traffic. Two continuous tracks probably mean only cars have used the runway, while three light ruts vanishing into unbroken snow cover reveal aircraft usage, and the more tracks there are on the snow surface, the better you can feel about your chances for a safe landing.

If you see no sign of activity, however, you had better not use the field. There must be a reason for the absence of clues and signs of life. It may be a foot of powdered snow! Attempting to land on a fresh snow surface is like playing Russian roulette with a derringer; the stuff may be only a couple of inches deep, or it may be a couple of feet. Take your chance and see what you get, a smooth rollout or an inverted airplane. Aside from uncertainty over the accumulation, depth perception ranges from slim to none over fresh snow. You could fly right into the ground on your approach, so land on unbroken snow only in an emergency.

Caring for Your Bird

The airplane requires careful preparation for a post-snowstorm flight, above and beyond the normal preflight inspection. If possible, remove the wheel fairings so they cannot accumulate snow and frozen slush. When the aircraft has been parked outside, plan to spend considerable time digging it out. If the first snow was melting as it fell, you may have a lift-destroying layer of rough ice on the wing surfaces, which must be removed before flight. A heated hangar, an alcohol spray, push brooms, and time to spare may all be required to cope with the snow-covered airplane.

Pay particular attention to openings in the aircraft where blowing snow may have entered. Uncovered cowlings can pack full, not only through the front openings but through the lower openings where the cooling air exits. Watch for snow accumulated in the carburetor heat inlet, where it can melt inflight to give your engine a diet of water. The air cleaner is invariably obstructed by packed snow. Remove loose snow from the insides of the control surfaces, and dig any obstructions out of the control surface gaps. Aircraft with stabilator tails require careful deicing to keep the balance of the flying tail unchanged. Inflight flutter can develop with an out-of-balance stabilator. Stabilators also require large openings in the aft fuselage, through which snow can enter in quantity. Make sure all drain holes are open, so a day of thawing temperatures won't leave you with a 50-pound block of ice in the tailcone on the morning after.

Taxi and Takeoff Technique

With the runway checked and the aircraft prepared, you are ready to do battle. During taxi, expect poor braking action on packed snow and more than adequate drag in areas of loose snow. Use full-up elevator when the airplane is moving to keep the nosegear light, or to keep the tailwheel down, depending on your type of landing gear. Avoid starting and stopping in deep loose snow, which can be picked up by the propeller and plug an air filter. Run up on a clear spot, if available, where the brakes can have a chance to hold.

The takeoff should be accomplished in the best soft-field style, using the recommended flap setting and lifting the nosewheel or tailwheel as soon as possible. It is important to keep the tail low in any case, just clear of the snow surface, both to gain maximum lift from the wings for an early liftoff and to minimize the tendency to nose over if a patch of deeper snow is encountered. Plan to use twice as much runway as normal, and choose a point at which you will discontinue the takeoff attempt if acceleration is poor. If a sluggish takeoff is aborted, you make another attempt more successful by holding to your previous tracks to pack a widened path when taxiing

Fig. 25-2. If the snow starts falling again, this airport may soon be closed once again. Drifts are forming downwind of old snowpiles, blocking nearly half the pavement.

118

back, which you can use for increased acceleration next time.

After liftoff, enjoy the view and relax. Retractable gear aircraft should have the gear operated through a few cycles to make sure all snow and sludge are dislodged before finally stowing the gear in the wells. There is much less clearance than most pilots realize, and numerous malfunctions have resulted when snow and ice have packed into wheel wells. Be prepared to change your navigation habits over a snow-covered landscape, because many familiar landmarks are altered or missing. A black roadway can be hidden beneath a snow blanket, town roofs blend into the landscape, section lines may be indistinct, and you will find yourself calling upon old compass skills.

Landing with the White Stuff

The landing, like the takeoff, is performed at the slowest possible speed, which normally means full flaps and stick all the way back for a full-stall touchdown from a foot or so above the runway. The rollout will be short if any appreciable snow is on the runway, so leave the stick full back after touchdown and rely on aerodynamic braking. Tailwheel airplanes should be plopped on tailwheel first if control permits, giving an anchor effect to help hold the tail down as the mainwheels touch the snow. If used carefully, a little throttle can hang the aircraft in the air for an even slower touchdown.

Okay, you're out of gas or being crowded by deteriorating weather and you feel you must land at an unused airfield with unknown snow depth. Try to define the runway limits; if runway lights are visible, remember there is normally 10 feet between the lights and the pavement's edge. Judgment of flare height will be a problem, and the lights can be of further help in this case. Other useful aids are bushes along the runway, boundary fences, and the like. If you have any dark, disposable items on board you could make a pass down the runway and drop them in the touchdown zone to give you some depth perception as you land. Have your passengers pad and brace themselves in case the snow is deeper than you have anticipated. Stall out just above the snow and hope for the best.

Winter flying can be beautiful, but don't be the first to land at a strange field. You may have to stay longer than you'd planned!

Part V
Using Your Head

Chapter 26
Judgment Call:
the Go/No-Go Decision

Recognizing the limitations of one's abilities and those of the airplane one flies is basic to the continued survival of any pilot. Yet, all too often we forget we have limitations until we are brought up short by exceeding them.

A broken airplane seldom comes about because of one simple incident. It usually takes a combination of factors, such as a dark night, a gusting crosswind, and a tired pilot, acting in concert, to make it happen. Even a mechanical failure can usually be prevented from becoming catastrophic if the pilot has enough knowledge of the airplane's systems to isolate or work around the problem. Safe flying starts with *knowledge*, so that the pilot will recognize what his equipment can and cannot do.

Acquisition of knowledge is an ongoing process, not merely a set of information to be learned with no further study needed. Aviation is a constantly changing business and, while the weather and the basic laws of flight are immutable, operational restraints and airplane handling procedures do change. The careful pilot will keep up with what's going on by reading the bulletin board, buying the AIM or J-Aid services, catching the local NOTAMS from a transcribed broadcast, and yes, subscribing to the aviation press. The pilot who gets his or her ticket and stops studying only goes downhill—with serious safety results.

Being Honest with Yourself

Honesty plays a large part in developing a pilot's judgment. You must recognize that there are things you can't do—or at least shouldn't do—even if other pilots are getting away with it. Attempting a zero-zero takeoff in fog may be practical for the alert, rested pilot who has hundreds of instrument hours in that particular cockpit, yet foolhardy for the tired, rusty, or inexperienced aviator in a strange airplane. Be honest with yourself. There aren't going to be any traffic cops standing at the airport to hold you back from killing yourself. You're going to have to say *no* to yourself—by yourself. And, when pressures of your business or family are involved, you had best be a pilot first and everything else second.

Regulations, you see, are quite vague about what is and isn't safe operation. This is because pilots vary widely in capability, as does their equipment, and the regs are weighty enough without adding a chapter and verse for each type of operation. The FARs provide only the sketchiest framework of guidelines. They must be supplemented by our own restraints to provide adequate margins of safety. What's SOP in New England just isn't smart in a Rocky Mountain meadow. IFR fuel reserves sufficient for the coastal regions had best be increased across the Great Plains. One may indulge in a bit more boldness when a glideslope receiver and marker beacon are installed, while a single-localizer setup demands higher weather minimums.

So we all have limitations. I venture to say no two pilots will have exactly the same set of guidelines; your own personal limits will vary from day to day. We all have those days when we wake up tired and perhaps are fighting off the leftover flu bug or the effects of last night's party. It doesn't make sense to tackle the same tough situation under these conditions as we might on a clearheaded day.

One of the most dangerous circumstances is an airplane with two pilots and no captain. When a pair of aviators are of roughly equal experience, neither wants to throw in the towel and admit defeat. Often the person at the controls will continue on in the face of doubtful odds, secretly wishing he could quit, while the individual on his right silently wishes he *would* quit. Remember, airplanes are not run by committee decisions. Don't let anyone—another pilot, the boss, a controller, *anyone*—pressure you into exceeding what you know are your proper limitations.

Arriving at Limitations

But how to arrive at a clear-cut decision about limitations—*that's* the question. Start by defining the mission. Is it a departure with no immediate need to return, or will it be necessary to come back later in the day? Will it be a strictly VFR trip, or do you feel capable of handling IFR conditions, in *this* airplane, in *this* area? Is there a hard-and-fast schedule to be met, necessitating alternate modes of transportation if the flight is scrubbed, or can there be more flexibility in departure and arrival times?

Having defined the mission, carefully consider the weather situation. If you don't understand the weather, don't fly in it. Ask the FSS specialist about the synopsis; match existing conditions with what was forecast, then consider whether or not you want to bet your life on what you've been told. If you have seen this type of weather situation before, in this same area, you may have a fair handle on what to expect aloft. On the other hand, if you're a stranger in a strange land, watch out, and don't push your limitations.

Weather limitations depend on the pilot's experience, equipment, time of day, terrain, and alternatives available. By all means, always have an alternate everywhere along the line. Instrument pilots aren't the only ones who need alternates. Whether IFR or VFR, it always pays to know where you can go if conditions deteriorate or an emergency occurs. Never leave yourself with no out. Knowing there is a nice warm airport a few minutes away helps avoid anxious moments and occasionally preserves an airplane.

Finally, after recognizing the task ahead and the weather to be faced, take a look at yourself and your equipment. You and the airplane are a team; neither can do the job alone. If you aren't feeling razor-sharp, keep out of tight weather and long, tiring flights. If the oil consumption is running a bit high, or the primary radio has been going to sleep occasionally, don't push yourself quite as far before yelling "WOA!" If it's your first trip in this machine, don't bet your life on the untested avionics or instrument lights.

What's Judgment?

Most accident reports show the pilot exercised poor judgment at some point in the flight, perhaps before he left the ground, enroute, or even at the last minute, just before the crunch. Judgment is not something you can buy, have subliminally implanted, or borrow from other people. It is something to be acquired from within yourself and it is absolutely vital for your survival. Kid yourself on the highway and you may get a ticket; lie to yourself in an airplane and you may get dead. Good judgment is simply recognizing that you do have limitations and resolving to stay within them. Poor judgment is allowing yourself to be swayed by the press of non-related forces to the point of compromising your limitations.

Good judgment is adding full fuel when it looks like the weather at the destination is falling apart. Poor judgment is pressing on because you need to be there and a fuel stop will take too long. Good judgment is driving a trip because the forecast wasn't proving out in the sequence reports, while poor judgment is launching off "just to see how it looks" when you know that doing so will almost certainly require you to continue the flight. Good judgment is waiting an hour for another set of sequences to come out; poor judgment is taking off without checking weather, figuring on picking it up enroute. Good judgment is asking a mechanic to look at something you suspect is a problem; poor judgment is putting it off until the airplane is in for annual in a month or two.

You can't inject judgment into a vacant mind. It comes from within, tempered by experience and knowledge. Don't ignore the reality of limitations, and strive to possess an airman's longevity insurance—good judgment.

Chapter 27

Slow Down to Save Time

At any time during the chain of events leading to an accident, the pilot involved could have taken action to prevent the mishap. Obviously, he or she did not. We who were not direct participants in the calamity often ask ourselves, "Why would a guy do that?" If the pilot is still around to give us an answer, he might very well say, "I was in a hurry and I just didn't take time to . . ."

Haste in the cockpit is ingrained into us from our initial hour of training, when emphasis was placed on "staying ahead of the airplane" lest the machine seize the opportunity to run amok. However, we must guard against taking satisfaction in the sheer rapidity of our movements around the cockpit. Like the rat running a maze, a pilot can be trained to manipulate controls habitually, and if the airplane or the situation strays from the routine, a pilot's conditioned responses may not be the correct ones. A few examples will bear out my hypothesis.

Habits Aren't Enough

A friend of mine who made a gear-up landing told me the accident was a matter of following habitual procedures. As he planned his departure before taking the runway, he intended to leave the gear down in the pattern. But after liftoff his hand went to the gear lever as it had for thousands of previous takeoffs. We can almost see his trained response bring up the gear, ease back the throttles, tweak the props into synch, and add a touch of nose-down trim, all by subconscious, learned action rather than by conscious thought. As he concentrated on the landing, that followed, he *knew* the gear was down because that's how he had planned it before takeoff. The result was a perfectly routine procedure right up until the prop blades hit the pavement.

The pilot's problems began with haste, the need to make a quick up-and-around pattern, which diverted attention from the matters at hand, such as confirming gear-down. The airplane was being superbly flown by trained reflexes right to the point of impact; he never recalled raising the gear, because his brain was not involved in the action.

Hasty, Wastey

That haste can make waste was brought home to me rather forcefully by my first multi-engine instructor several years ago. We were shooting touch-and-goes, and I was getting good at it. Every touchdown was followed by the same pattern: power up, flags up, gear up, climbout, and blueline. We were flying an early Aero Commander with main gear that simply swiveled aft for retraction, and my automatic touch-and-go responses had gotten so quick that I'd unlocked the gear and moved the handle while we were still on the runway. As the old Commander began to settle the foot or so between its belly and the surface, my instructor hauled the yoke back in his lap to keep us airborne and delivered one of the few curses I ever heard him utter. "Don't get in such a big ******* hurry; take some time to fly the airplane" was the gist of his stinging lecture. My quick hands in the cockpit were not a virtue, they were a vice.

Even during moments of stress, take your time. Remember, if you have only one chance to get out of an emergency, take a second to make sure you're doing the right thing. All too many times a hot-rock multi-engine pilot, faced with an engine-out emergency, has hastily pulled his levers, zip, zip, zip—and feathered the wrong engine. Yes, something needs to be done, but it has to be the *right* something, or you're not going to make it through the darkness to the other end of the tunnel.

Get Your Priorities in the Right Order

Whenever the situation demands positive, immediate action, you should establish priorities. You can't do everything at once, so take care of first things first. An instrument student making a missed-approach will often bring in a touch of power, raise the nose a bit, and grab for the microphone while the aircraft is still settling, anxious to get his report out of the way. Forget the radio for a few seconds, until you have first set the power, stabilized the climbout attitude, and, perhaps, begun the turn toward the missed-approach fix, if an immediate change in heading is required. Then tell the tower you've missed, on the odd chance that they haven't already seen your pull-up.

Even the basics of airmanship require a certain amount of patience, a trait not always compatible with our desire to execute the privileges of pilot-in-command. A fast level-off from a climb, coupled with a quick power reduction and trim adjustment, will result in several hundred feet of altitude sinking away, all because the pilot didn't give the airplane time to accelerate. It may be an unfamiliar combination of high density altitude and heavy load that causes the airplane to be a little slow in coming up onto the step, but whatever the cause, the pilot should have been watching and feeling his airplane, instead of trying to play up-tempo music on the cockpit controls.

Stay with the Airplane

There is a limit to an airplane's capacity to produce, and you should pace your actions accordingly. Even if you're trained to the point of lightning-quick moves, keep your brain engaged to make sure the airplane is keeping up with you. Don't pull the power and prop back to a reduced climb power just as soon as the airplane breaks ground; give the VSI time to build and grab a little altitude first. Even if you have noise-sensitive neighbors off the end of the runway, leaving the power alone for a few seconds and holding V_y speed will result in less perceptible noise impact than augering across their rooftops at low altitude into a flat climb.

Trying too hard just invites negative results. Back when I was beginning to learn the rudiments of glider flying, I would wrap the sailplane into a 60° bank at a minimum-sink speed, trying to stay in the hot core of a thermal. I usually wound up flying in and out of the stall burble, generating more sink through drag than the lift of the rising air could offset. An old-timer showed me how to do it, with a less aggressive technique: Maintain more airspeed or use a shallower bank to avoid the stall burble, and milk the overall thermal until you can gradually shift into the core. Even a little climb is better than a sink.

The biggest difference observed in flying with a truly experienced pilot—a wise old bird with years, not just hours, logged in the air—is the relaxed way he uses the controls. As you watch such a person fly, you see no wasted motion, no doubling back to correct lost altitude, no resetting of trim due to a hasty move. This pilot has learned to wait and watch the machine, giving it *what* it needs, exactly *as much* as it needs, just *when* it needs it, not before and not after. It doesn't matter that he has never flown this type of airplane over this route before; give him a few minutes to settle into place and he'll find out how to get what he wants from the airplane, with patience. If the situation is complex, he will probably ask you to answer the radio or look for an approach plate; he's setting priorities, and the airplane always comes first.

We can hear the distinction of experience each time we fly by analyzing radio technique. A newly rated eager beaver pilot blurts out his call-up or readback at 150 words per minute with gusts to 200, a method that is sure to generate a "Say again" from the controller. The older, wiser heads will talk at a rate compatible with the traffic situation, endeavoring to get his information across on the first transmission to save time in the long run. Strive to eliminate unneeded verbiage from your transmission, but keep your speed of delivery slow enough that a controller won't have to ask for a repeat or, worse yet, possibly misunderstand your intentions. Take a moment to listen after coming on a new frequency before transmitting; just because you were told to report on 122.55 doesn't mean it has to be done and completed within a two-second void period.

By all means, stay awake in the cockpit, but make your actions studied and purposeful rather than just quick for quickness' sake. Fly in a state of relaxed alertness, establishing priorities to handle the busy times but never letting your hands run ahead of your brain. It takes less time in the long run and the airplane will be flown more professionally. You will wind up staying truly ahead of the airplane, thanks to the time saved by eliminating wasted motion.

Chapter 28

Stress Management

Everybody talks about stress and how it affects people; let's see how stress can influence a pilot. A little stress can be a healthy challenge, but a lot of stress can be tiresome. Excessive stress can be life-threatening. Nearly all contemporary lifestyles contain stressful situations, and as modern-day pilots we are subject to considerable stress as a result of our endeavors.

Flying isn't always stressful. As we all know, boring holes in the serenity of the sky, far above one's earthly troubles, can be a soothing way to shed a burdensome load of cares. Unfortunately, we late-20th-Century types ruin a good thing by building additional stress into it. We often attempt to put our aerial toys to work as tools of transportation, which is a fine example of having our cake and eating it, too. But coping with the age-old perils of the sky while trying to adhere to a schedule is like turning up the heat under a pressure boiler.

Were it not for the effect of stress on their flying, we wouldn't concern ourselves with pilots who try to fly from Point A to Point B on a timetable. But when a person's ability to function effectively as a pilot breaks down as a result of his or her stress overload, it's time to look at the problem and see if there is a solution. For instance, if a pilot lost most of the preceding night's sleep worrying about whether or not he would make it to the big meeting tomorrow, he won't fly as well as he might were he well-rested. As another example, the pressure to get home in time to punch the clock on Monday morning is just the sort of stress that has buried more than a few families when common sense gave way to unrestrained urgency.

Shedding Stress

Let's try to understand what goes on in the pilot's mind when a flying problem arises; then we'll see if we can "unload" this highly stressful situation.

Psychologists say people handle threatening problems in one of two ways, both of which are quite effective. One way is to ignore the whole thing and block it out of the mind completely. It is particularly appropriate when there really isn't any individual action that can be taken to solve the problem. Averting a major war is a good example. You say, "It's out of my hands, so I just won't worry about it," and by dismissing it from your conscious thoughts it ceases to be a source of worry.

The second method of coping with a threat is to take all possible precautions in preparing for it, thus relieving yourself of uncertainty by saying, "There, I'm ready; let it come." Averting fears of a major war in this way might mean hoarding a year's supply of food or selling stocks in vulnerable industries. Both types of reaction can be carried to ridiculous extremes, but they are typical of how we handle daily life.

In flying, you can't ignore all problems very well, but you can ignore the ones you can't do anything about. If you are 500 miles away from home and really want to start back, but one member of your party isn't going to be ready to leave until tomorrow, you may as well stop worrying. You're not going anywhere. Staring out the

Fig. 28-1. Stress on the pilot can mean stress on the airplane. This Navion's pilot forgot his wheels until he was nearly down; a last-minute go-around flattened the prop tips.

window won't do anything to hurry up the departure, so put the flight out of your mind and enjoy whatever pleasures the local attractions have to offer.

From the beginning of flight training, you are instructed to leave nothing to chance. Flying is a terribly unforgiving occupation to those who make dumb mistakes. Therefore, taking appropriate precautions would seem to be the more useful reaction in a highly-stressful situation. This increases your workload and spoils the fun of a spontaneous flight, but it must be done if you're to avoid dangerous situations that could create even more stress.

Preflight Stress Relief

Let's divide our actions into two areas, actions related to preflight preparations and actions undertaken in flight. As you approach a trip that has been scheduled for some time, stress mounts up naturally. Will the weather be up to your minimums? Will the airplane you have reserved get back on time? Is there enough daylight to get there before dark? Can you afford to miss another day of work if you don't get back? And so forth.

This set of circumstances brings us to the old go/no-go decision. How you handle this stress-maker depends on how closely you have to adhere to the flight plan. Perhaps the time of departure isn't so critical, if the airplane isn't rented for a specific block of hours. If the weather is bad in the morning, leave in the afternoon. If you can't get organized in time to make it today, fly tomorrow. Tell everybody involved that's the way you're going to play the game and you can stop worrying about the timetable.

Even the destination need not be cast in concrete. If you've promised the kids a ride to West Point and you're fretting about the forecast in that direction, plan an equally entertaining trip in another direction for the little dears, and cease that pacing back and forth to the window. By going one step further with a third, ground-bound plan that you can press into service if all flying must be scrubbed, you no longer have anything to get uptight about, having covered every eventuality.

But what about those *really* important trips, the ones you've just *got* to make? They're sure to cause ulcers unless you assess the situation realistically. No means of transporation is fluke-proof, and that goes especially for general aviation. Even the airlines occasionally must cancel flights because of weather or mechanical malfunctions. If the trip is important, simply set up another means of getting there if you're not able to fly as planned—fill the car up with gas, make an airline reservation, hire an instrument-rated pilot, or arrange a rain date. When you've done everything you can, go to sleep and forget about it.

If you can make some preparation to deal with interfering problems, do so. If you can't do anything more, forget it! Worry never parted the clouds or calmed a crosswind. For the must-be-there trips, set up a final decision time—the last possible moment when you could switch to the car or run to catch the airliner. If your path is not clear as that hour approaches, switch to your alternate and don't look back. I've driven a lot of miles while cursing the sunshine overhead, but my decision time had come when the clouds were still thick. If you don't have the minimums you need, *don't fly*. Never believe a forecast until it starts to happen.

Inflight Stress Relief

Okay, you've taken every possible precaution before getting into the air. Now you're airborne and a different sort of stress sets in. Flying is a time-sensitive game; you have to be *somewhere* before the fuel runs out and you must keep tabs on your progress to see if you'll make it. Before takeoff, the passage of time was only an inconvenience, not a threat. In the air, time is of paramount importance.

Determine the source of any inflight stress you feel building. If you're concerned about the sound of the engine, note the readings of the temperature and pressure gauges and check them periodically. No change usually means no problem. Troubleshoot by switching mags, trying the carb heat, and adjusting the mixture. Then quit worrying. If the situation deteriorates, just head for that alternate airport you've always got in mind. Be confident that you can handle the problem in an organized way, and stress can be managed.

Is the weather enroute different from that forecast? That's a stress-maker as old as aviation. Get hold of Flight Watch on 122.0 and find out where the weather is still good; there's your out. Then check to see if the observations ahead are up to your standards. If they aren't, you've just made a decision to divert, *regardless* of how important the trip may be. Remember, "must-fly" trips lose that status the moment you're airborne. You should always divert if safety demands it. Because you've done all you can, ignore the stress of missed meetings or cancelled appointments. If the weather falls apart, don't risk your life to preserve a business schedule.

Never let stress build to the point of interfering with the rational thinking necessary for flying; doing so just *invites* an accident because the airplane lacks a coherent pilot. One corporation I am familiar with has a simple rule for its businessmen-pilots: If they are not comfortable with their flight situation, they are to put the airplane on the ground and work out their schedule in the airport lounge. That attitude saves a lot of lives by allowing the pilot to shed stress like a dog shaking off water. We should all adopt that policy.

Chapter 29

Being Considerate

There was a time when pilots could fly pretty much as they pleased. As long as they stayed within the regulations, any public nuisance resulting from their actions could be smoothed over by the offer of a free ride. After all, pilots were supermen, to be given a trifle more slack than ground-bound mortals.

Alas, those halcyon days are gone. Your pilot's license now scores few points at a cocktail party ("Oh, really? Then you must know my brother-in-law; he flies, too"), and it has almost no armoring effect against the slings and arrows of outraged citizenry. As Rodney Dangerfield says, we don't get no respect. We're going to have to consider the effect of our actions, as perceived by others, if we want to count on the public's support in the clinches.

Departing Graciously

Consideration of others begins with the start-up. Strive for a low-rpm light-off and warm-up; 800 rpm will keep an alternator on the line and hold a little suction pressure for the gyros, and it will move a lot less dirt than 1200 rpm and keep the ramp quieter, as well. When taxiing, use minimum power and brake to get the bird to the runup area, and leave the strobes off so onlookers won't be blinded. A 1500-rpm taxi adds to engine wear, shortens brake life, and is generally regarded as a sign of a poor pedigree. Then too, passengers usually don't care for squealing, swerving, high-speed taxi runs.

Limit your use of power to the few seconds necessary for mags, suction, and prop tests; it's amazing how far the sound of a runup will carry on a still summer evening. If you have first-time passengers on board, keep them informed about the sequence of events without alluding to impending doom; explain that the pre-takeoff checks are done to make sure everything is in perfect working order. Do not say things like "If this mag quits the other one will bring us home" or "Looks like that'll be enough fuel." Exude confidence. Oddly enough, most new passengers don't like to see the captain perusing a checklist ("Can't he even remember what he's supposed to do?"), so use it but keep it unobtrusive.

Brief your passengers on what will be happening before you kick in the afterburner. Tell them it will be somewhat noisier than a car, that a turn will follow the liftoff, and that any low-level turbulence will be topped shortly. Take a good, vigilant look for traffic, even if you have a controller's blessing. If operating uncontrolled, don't pull out in front of an airplane on short final or close-in base leg unless you're in contact with the pilot; the FARs give the landing aircraft priority for very good reasons. You may precipitate a go-around even though you feel there's plenty of room.

When using the radio, think about the other fellow. Check that you have the volume turned up before you talk, and don't start blasting away right after dialing up the channel; listen for a second or two, in case there's a comeback in progress. If you have manual squelch, open it up a little on the first contact to make sure it isn't filtering out a distant reply then adjust it after you raise the tower. Think before you talk, don't compose on the air, and avoid non-productive conversation.

Keeping the Peace

More public ire is raised over departure procedures than any other flight operation. If there is a preferred takeoff path, use it. If there isn't create one; flying low over housing developments usually can be avoided. If an extended straight-out will get you around the edge of town, maintain the runway heading. Comply with the tower's wishes if the controllers express any preferences, but go further than that; in the interest of future harmony, watch for noise-sensitive areas on your own. For instance, I frequent one uncontrolled airport that gets a fair amount of jet traffic and 90 percent of the big-iron drivers might make a right turn out, smack-dab over the town square, because that's the logical way to head for the VOR. The management should pass the word, but doesn't because it's afraid of hurting Big Dome's feelings. If John Q. Public gets riled enough, Big Dome may find that airport gone someday, so a word to the wise would be in order.

Departure technique should place as much altitude under the airplane as possible, as quickly as possible, to minimize the exposure

134

at high power settings. Some pilots mistakenly use partial power for takeoff, or reduce power abruptly after liftoff, attempting to lessen noise. The result may be exactly the opposite; reduced power means less altitude will be gained by the runway end, and as the edge of town is reached the neighbors get a big dose of pistons swapping holes. As long as your passengers can tolerate the high deck angle, rotate on schedule to achieve V_y at 50 feet and leave the power at full bore for a minute or so, hanging the airplane on the prop to leave the airport vertically rather than horizontally. No certified engine will be harmed by this short full-power run; as a matter of fact, engines sometimes wait for the first power reduction before coming unglued, so there is every reason to leave the throttle alone for a while.

I would make one exception to my wide-open rule, for airplanes powered by the 300-hp Continental IO-520, rated at 2850 rpm for five minutes; that big howler rattles the dishes halfway to Cucamonga as the prop tips go supersonic. If I owned one, I would have a mark inscribed on the prop vernier shaft so I could limit takeoff rpm to 2700 unless the strip were super-short. Only 15 hp is lost by derating the engine thusly, not a significant amount in normal operation. Keeping the prop speed down hopefully will hold the neighbor's temper down, as well.

The maximum-rate climbout should be held for the first 1000 feet of altitude, at which time a gradual transition is made to a more customary climb angle. If this can be done within the airport boundary, the initial power reduction will be made before overflying any residential areas. Should there be no alternative to departing over those poorly placed houses surrounding small airports, make the reduction from takeoff to climb power as soon as you think it safe—perhaps at the end of the runway.

Airplanes with fixed-pitch propellers seldom need power reductions for climb, as they customarily are equipped with cruising propellers that limit rpm to well below redline at low airspeed. Airplanes with constant-speed propellers are typically given a power setting of about 80 percent for climbout; prop speed is the critical factor in controlling noise, and at elevations above 4000 feet MSL, the throttle need not be pulled back before the prop control, as manifold pressure will not be greater than 24 inches in most normally aspirated engines.

Common courtesy dictates that you inform the control tower of your desired direction of flight when you report ready, so the staff can plan accordingly. At uncontrolled airports, taking a shortcut onto course by angling around into the touch-and-go pattern is poor manners; if you can't gain enough altitude to clear the pattern, you should swing out a mile or so.

Enroute Niceties

Consideration of others continues in the enroute phase of the flight; don't assume your passengers are capable of the same bladder-busting enduros you can make. For the nonveterans, a two-hour hop is plenty long enough, and even that should be cut short in turbulent conditions. Try for smooth air for your passenger's sake, both in timing of the flight to avoid the roughest part of the day and in choice of cruising altitude.

Don't be guilty of drifting upward a few hundred feet at a time with the rising turbulence level; breaking the odd /even cruising altitude rule can easily result in a head-on conflict at a closing speed of 300 mph, so if you're going up, make it a full 2000-foot change. If your airplane ascends in an extremely nose-high attitude, break up the climb with shallow turns, both to clear the airspace ahead for oncoming traffic and to create movement in the other pilot's field of view.

As you progress along your route, note significant unreported weather and make a pilot report to Flight Watch. Your report may save someone else from wasting fuel when the pass is closing rapidly, and knowing a clearing-line's position can ease a worried pilot's mind. If we keep such information to ourselves, everyone will have to discover the truth separately.

Remember to put as much thought into the arrival as you did the departure. By planning the letdown, you can leave the power at a low cruise setting when you level off for the traffic pattern, instead of dragging along at cruise power after letting down early. To eliminate the snarl of redlining rpm, don't run a constant-speed prop into low pitch until the power is reduced for approach.

Arrival Courtesy

Get your communications act together early in the game, listening to ATIS or the tower's chatter to get the numbers, then checking in at a well-defined reporting point. Keep all conversations short, whether with tower, FSS or Unicom, but talk slowly enough to preclude misunderstandings. Double-check your choice of frequencies, most particularly at uncontrolled fields; know whether to use the closed-tower frequency, FSS traffic advisory, Unicom or Multicom.

Bear in mind the needs of others during the approach phase of the flight; if you see traffic holding for departure, fly a short approach rather than take a grand tour of the countryside, so the pilot on the ground can get his overheating engine into the air. Try for a turnoff at the first intersection to eliminate the need for a 180 on the runway. If you have traffic following, keep your speed up as long as possible and clear the runway promptly; creating a go-around situation needlessly is poor manners. Never, *never* make a right-hand pattern just for your own convenience at an uncontrolled field with standard patterns.

Use some discretion when parking your bird; the lineman may be busy when you wander onto the ramp, if such a person is employed, casting you on your own devices. Pick a spot that lines up with the other airplanes and doesn't block hangars, taxiways, or the fuel pits. Before you run off to town, hunt up an official personage and ask if it's okay to park there for the appropriate length of time. You may be occupying someone's private slot with passion-pink wheel chocks and custom-fitted tiedown ropes.

Your consideration of others encourages the kind of discipline needed to make you a superior pilot. The aviator who charges ahead without regard to the effect of his own actions probably will bring himself to grief someday, due to the lack of restraint in his personal flying habits. Be a decent sort; it'll improve everyone's frame of mind and make you a better pilot.

Chapter 30

Doing Stupid Things Sensibly

In aviation, as in all fields of endeavor, some things are just not discussed in school. Training texts will contain pat, cut-and-dried answers to specific questions, leaving students to learn later in their careers that some situations just don't fit the textbook examples. Checkrides are passed by reciting the standard catechism drilled into the novitiate's head by curriculum-bound instruction. The FAA handbooks and manufacturers' approved manuals simply ignore nonstandard, deviate behavior, assuming that no one will ever stray from the straight-and-narrow. Alas, there will come a day when an emboldened young aviator will wonder "What if . . . " and, because he was never told specifically why he shouldn't experiment, he may try some forbidden act just to see what happens. And *that* my friends, is an open invitation to disaster.

But Why Not?

We live in a questioning, testing age. Today's educators are encouraging students to ask "Why" or "Why not," and if no one can give them what they consider to be a straight answer, they are encouraged to attempt to find out for themselves. This may be healthy, but it can lead to a lot of bruises in the course of experimentation. The point is, we can expect the current crop of young pilots to try some stupid things, just like yesterday's pilots did. We can only hope that they won't ignore common sense.

Let me be the first to disclaim any intentions of encouraging illegal or unsafe acts. Hopefully, all pilots will refrain from stepping outside the guidelines of safe operation as set forth in the regulations and approved flight manuals. However, there is a real world, where aviation exists as a self-regulated activity for the most part, all the carefully worded regulations not withstanding. To protect the interests of their employers, government bureaucrats and company lawyers will write only broad, generalized statements containing simple restrictions with no incriminating illumination.

When an airplane is placarded "intentional spins prohibited," its pilot has no way of knowing if the aircraft was found to be unstable at some point during the spin, if it would recover safely but not quickly enough to satisfy certification requirements, or it the manufacturer simply didn't want to assume the liability of endorsing spins. So if a pilot is feeling his or her oats someday, and decides to try a spin, the outcome may be very much in doubt. But human nature being what it is, a blanket prohibition is just not enough to restrain some bold but unknowledgable individuals.

It is foolish to expect the situation regarding specific information to improve; society is advancing ever deeper into a "sue thy neighbor" philosophy, and open honesty has now become so unexpected as to be suspect in itself. Therefore, pilots bent on survival must look beyond the letter of the law as written and apply the timeless guidance of common sense. We are going to examine some less-than-legal operations that are often undertaken, officially sanctioned or not, and will try to offer sensible restraints to the pilots bent on self-destruction.

Boondocks Operation

Consider the off-airport landing—legal, but it just isn't done, right? Well, a little observation reveals that it *is* being done—by bush pilots, glider pilots, crop dusters, and a few thrill-seekers. After all, it doesn't take too many touchdowns on some poorly maintained dirt strips that are officially recognized as airports to convince a pilot that a cow pasture can't be much worse. So the next time our pilot decides to visit Uncle Ben's farm, he or she may try landing on the back forty. Having gotten away with it once, the pilot is likely to try it again and again, until finally coming to grief.

Rather than expressing disapproval of all landings on unpaved surfaces, as is the usual practice during training, let's apply common sense. Off-airport landing are 1) terribly rough on airplanes, particularly the more modern designs; 2) risky, much like driving at night with your headlights off; and 3) probably outside the coverage of your insurance policy. Therefore, when considering operating from anything other than a regularly used airport, you should first *walk* the entire surface, not just drive over it or fly over it, and certainly you should not take anyone's word for its condition. Count your paces to verify the length and look at every square foot of the area to be used; it only takes *one* unseen rock or gopher hole to ruin your day. If you decide to land there, at least you'll know what you're getting into. Use common sense and you'll probably find yourself sticking to normal airports.

Illegal Aerobatics

Now on to another subject seldom discussed, merely forbidden: acrobatic flight in normal-category airplanes. Ground school prohibitions quickly forgotten, a new pilot soon discovers that 1) ordinary utility and normal category airplanes are perfectly capable of being flown into some unusual attitudes, especially if entry speeds well above maneuvering speed are used, and 2) it sure is a lot of fun to see the horizon from all those different angles. Unfortunately, every so often someone takes an airplane apart trying to prove he's as good as Bob Hoover, little knowing that Bob Hoover wouldn't dream of attempting his routine without a lot of careful experimentation first.

Again, use some common sense. If you're going to throw an airplane around, you need lots of altitude, a very strong machine, and some training in recoveries from unusual attitudes. It makes no difference that the self-taught aerobat may have gotten away with a flip-flop or two in a stock machine; eventually he or she will lose control and fall out of a maneuver, possibly exceeding the airplane's stress limits. At the least, a bad scare will be experienced; at the worst, the pilot will wake up dead. Common sense should restrict you from attempting aerobatics in stock flying machines, even if you choose to ignore the regulations.

The Buzz Job

Next, I'd like to see the hands of all those who have never buzzed a friend's house to let them know you were in the area. I thought so.

It clearly states in the regulations that we will not fly lower than 500 feet AGL, except over open water or vacant desert, yet most of us have been tempted into sneaking a fast pass down over the girlfriend's house, possibly getting away with it often enough to make it a habit. Buzzing is both risky and illegal, but if you're going to do it, use some common sense.

Don't loiter around sightseeing at low altitude. Make a cruise-speed dive, pull out over the objective, and get back up to a reasonable altitude immediately, in case the engine should pick that moment to pack up. Don't go down behind the trees or outbuildings — that isn't going to impress anyone but the grim reaper. Stay well above any obstructions. Don't let the airspeed drop below normal climb speed, and avoid cropduster turns down on the deck. One pass should be sufficient for a day's thrill, if you're determined to show off your boneheadedness. Remember, a lot of non-flying people are negatively impressed by a buzz job, and they've got the votes to ground us if their ire is sufficiently raised.

Flying Tanked

Next, let's talk about booze and flying. Never going to fly while under the influence, are we? The only problem is deciding when we're under the influence. A person wrapped in a warm alcoholic glow is hardly the one to determine his own fitness to fly, yet he's the one doing the deciding in nearly every case. The regulation specifying eight hours from bottle to throttle is only marginally better than no guideline at all, because it makes no allowance for the rate and amount of consumption or for body weight, all of which affect sobriety.

The fact is, there's no such thing as too little alcohol to have an effect. Whenever alcohol is consumed, there is always a depressing effect, which is enhanced by altitude. Even *one* beer or cocktail robs you of a portion of your faculties, unbeknownst to you, so only your common sense of self-restraint will prevent you from flying while under the influence. Don't trust your judgment after you've already imbibed. If flying is a major part of your life, you may want to seriously consider becoming a teetotaler, substituting the joys of flying for drinking, if you will. By staying on the wagon, you'll improve your chances for a long flying career, avoiding possible heart, liver, and brain damage. If you insist on maintaining what has come to be accepted as an active social use of alcohol, avoid any flying on the "morning after." Stay on the ground for 12 hours after moderate drinking, to be more safe, and for 24 hours following a real elbow-bender. Remember, common sense isn't likely to be working when you're slightly juiced, so make your decisions now.

A Little Something Extra

Overloading is yet another dark area normally left untouched by training. Even the most inexperienced student can't quite believe that an airplane will refuse to lift off if it is merely one pound over gross, but he is seldom told how much might be gotten away with in terms of overloading. When entering the real world he is forced to decide for himself when to offload fuel or baggage to maintain safety—at one pound over gross, 10, 20, when? The reasons for avoiding overload are well-known from ground school—the landing gear structure may be overstressed, operating limitations are more easily exceeded, and the performance charts for the aircraft become so much worthless paper. However, from a practical standpoint, few pilots are going to get excited about a five-pound overload.

So how much is *too* much? New pilots often ask, "A 10 percent overload beyond gross weight is all right, isn't it?" *No, it isn't.* Even 5 percent will noticeably degrade an aircraft's performance; on a 2500-pound airplane, that would be an extra 125 pounds. Unless the situation is an emergency, requiring a compromise to avoid greater risks from another source, 1 or 2 percent of gross weight is quite enough overload to ask the airplane to carry.

There are any number of other gray areas where the pilot's judgment must fill in gaps between regulations. As previously stated, aviation is largely self-regulated, and if you want to do something stupid, there are few constraints other than your common sense. Please, if you feel an overpowering urge to throw caution to the winds, research the matter first to find out why the regulations or limitations prohibit such an act. Then listen to your common sense, rather than the siren song of temptation.

Chapter 31

Are You Current?

Every so often someone asks me if I'm current in a Comanche, or a 310, or a SeaBee, or just about anything. While I seldom give a straight yes-or-no answer, tending to indulge in replies of "More or less," I have come to wonder just what they would really expect a normal airplane-hungry pilot to say. If you were being given a chance to fly an airplane of your heart's desire, and you thought you had a reasonable chance of getting it up and down without bending anything, wouldn't you probably say "Sure, I'm current"? I mean, who's going to say they're *not* current when there's flying to be done?

A case in point began with a phone call I received several years back. A chance acquaintance had left his Aztec weathered in at my field, and after continuing on to his destination and tending to business, he needed his bird in a hurry. Could I bring it down to him, if I was current in an Aztec? Heck yes, I'm current, I mean, sure, let's go. You get the picture. What I said was, "I'll be there in an hour, if I can get it started." My previous Aztec experience was a demo flight two years earlier, a total of half an hour, but I remembered the airplane as being docile and straightforward, and I saw no problem.

Bear in mind that I was doing nothing illegal; I was multi-rated, there were no passengers, it was strictly a gratis, VFR ferry flight. His banker and /or insurance company would have no doubt been uneasy, but I felt confident that I could make the short hop because I had done considerable homework on Aztecs and there was no weather or darkness problem. All went well, he was happy to get his airplane, and I was glad to get the time.

When Are You Current?

Now, back to the original question: *When are you current?* That depends on how demanding the flying is to be. After thousands of hours in a Cessna 150 /152, I feel reasonably sure of myself in one of those airplanes, and I could probably do about anything I wanted to with full peace of mind. But an airplane that I have only had an opportunity to fly a couple of hours is still not part of me, and I would consequently restrict my operations until I had more experience. So currency is up to the individual, depending on circumstances.

The FAA, wisely recognizing that both pilots and airplanes differ widely in their qualifications and abilities, stays pretty far away from this question of currency. To be legally current, the pilot must be rated in the category and class of aircraft, have his medical and flight review in order, and have high-performance airplane experience if he's flying an over-200-horsepower or retractable-gear airplane. If he wants to carry passengers, he needs three landings in the same category and class within the preceding 90 days. That's it; the rest is up to common sense.

The rules have to be flexible, because they must be written to cover all airmen. If we sought a regulation that would prevent a low-time pilot from jumping into an unfamiliar airplane in the middle of the night and flying into hard-IFR weather, it would also unduly restrict an experienced pilot who hasn't flown recently from using a simple airplane for a local pleasure hop. Further, some 250-hour pilots are worthy of the utmost trust, while some 3000-hour aviators are dangerously overconfident and underskilled. There is a limit to the number of laws one can write and still expect to have them obeyed. In most cases, the owner's insurance company will take over where the FAA leaves off, and the keeper of the airplane's keys ought to go even further when setting forth restrictions on the airplane's use.

Therefore, in answering that question about "Are you current?", you had best counter with "Current for what?" A test hop around the local area, or a 1000-mile cross-country trip? Nobody can make you suddenly, magically, current for every operation the airplane is capable of; only the passage of time while strapped to the seat cushion of the airplane can do that. You can lie your way into an airplane if you want, but it's your behind that's on the line when you can't handle the situation, so it pays not to overstate your qualifications.

Start on the Ground

Okay, let's make you current enough to fly a strange airplane in VFR daylight conditions, then proceed into IFR /night flying later.

Everybody wants to charge right out and get into the air, figuring that's the way to get current in a new bird. *Not so fast*. Those days are over; flying the airplane is now the *simple* part. Before you ever start the engine you need to spend an evening poring over the airplane's handbook and papers, making sure you have a working knowledge of the systems and recommended procedures. Then sit in the cockpit for a good long while, learning the position of controls and indicators with the handbook in your lap.

Find a good check pilot, CFI or not, who knows the airplane well; pick his brain for all it's worth. A CFI will have the advantage of being used to implanting procedures into empty minds, but he has to know what he's talking about before he can do that. With your preflight study, you should be a fertile field for such oral instruction.

The actual period of flying time necessary to make you competent to fly an airplane as pilot-in-command varies all over the place. If you have never flown anything but a Cherokee 140 in your entire 75-hour career, and that has been a year ago, trying to check out in a Cessna 182 is going to take a while. On the other hand, if you have 1000 hours of bonafide time and are regularly switching around in Cessnas from 172s to 210s, climbing into a strange 182 is no big deal, since you already know how Cessna does things. One gets used to changing mounts after a while, quickly finding the benchmarks of any new airplane to make an easy transition, but it's an acquired skill. (A note to such seasoned and confident switchers: Don't get too complacent, for they do change things on you, like using knots on the airspeed indicator or putting in a 100-octane engine instead of an 80-octane one.)

A checklist is vital to the transitioning aviator; without one, it is all too easy to omit some vital preflight check in the heat of battle, such as setting the directional gyro. However, after running the handbook's checklist, make a double-check of common items from your own memory (fuel, controls, instruments, trim, etc.) to make sure an unfamiliar checklist didn't lead you astray.

Take It Easy

Naturally, for the trial flight you should select a day without wind or weather problems. Keeping the loading light and well within CG limits is also important. A liftoff speed is selected, based on the stall speeds quoted in the handbook, and a rotation will be made just before reaching that figure, without actually trying to pull the airplane off. Let it run until it's ready to fly, then accelerate to best rate-of-climb speed after breaking ground. Just hold a heading and fly for the first few seconds—don't be in a big hurry to cut the power back or retract the gear and flaps. Keep up with the airplane and make all adjustments with a little forethought.

A 500-fpm cruise-climb is usually desirable after the initial departure, going up to 3000 feet AGL or more before leveling off to experiment with the airplane. Keep a watch on temperature gauges and other vital signs to become familiar with the powerplant's performance. When leveling off into cruise, leave the power up for a few minutes to build up speed quickly, then make final trim and power adjustments for cruise. Note the sight picture over the nose in a level-flight attitude, then roll into some good medium-banked 360° turns to see if you can get the feel of keeping altitude by eyeball.

Slow flight is next, starting with a clean airplane. Work down to the point of the stall warner's indication, then, using little or no power, try a straight-ahead stall to ascertain the minimum flying speed and the aircraft's stall characteristics. Don't prolong the stall; recover promptly, at least until you are sure the airplane has no bad habits. Lower the flaps and/or landing gear and perform the same slow-flight and approach-to-stall drill. Add 30 percent to the stall speeds observed in clean and dirty configurations, and make these 1.3 V_s figures your minimum flying speeds until you have gained familiarity with the airplane.

Take time to cover all aspects of the airplane's systems while in an actual flight environment. Try leaning procedures to see how much the mixture knob comes back; find out where the emergency gear-down handle is located; see if the radios are operable and accurate. If an autopilot is installed, try all modes to see if you understand its operation. Look around to see where the airplane's blind spots are located so you can be especially watchful for traffic approaching from that direction.

First Landing

Coming back down, find a comfortable power setting for a 500-fpm descent at cruise speed and trim, and make the proper airspeed reductions before dropping the gear or flaps. One-and-a-half times stall speed should be a comfortable traffic pattern speed; plan on having a good long final approach to give yourself time to get squared away before touching down. Stabilize the approach at 1.3 V_{s_0}, then reduce power cautiously as the ground comes up to avoid falling through a flare with a heavy, unfamiliar airplane. Wait out any ballooning tendencies and ease the stick back slowly in small increments; never get into a pushing and tugging match with a strange airplane on landing. If things get out of hand, give it full power and start all over again.

Brake cautiously, once down, in case the airplane is resting only lightly on its feet and a wheel tends to lock up. Keep the stick full back during the rollout, and raise flaps when all their effectiveness is diminished, making sure you move the right control. Shoot more landings until you are either satisfied or disgusted, but do make them full-stop if at all possible; touch-and-goes do not give the full range of changing control pressures and can put the new pilot behind the airplane if he's not alert. Try various flap settings and power combinations during landings, seeing what works best for this particular airplane. Some aircraft need power right down to the ground; others float eternally if power-off dissipation of speed isn't complete before entering ground effect.

Having proved your prowess, taxi back to the tiedown and shut down, securing the aircraft against wind or prop blast. *Now* are you current? Hardly; you've just proved you can keep the airplane from biting you under ideal conditions. It is up to you to get out and fly the bird until you are thoroughly familiar, then try it out under less-than-perfect wind or loading situations. After much more experience, go on to IFR and night operations, when you are utterly sure of your equipment and your mastery over same.

When are you current? When you have ceased to be surprised by something the airplane does, or doesn't do, not before. Let's face it, we can never be truly current enough in a flock of airplanes, but we should resolve to make every flight a step toward ultimate mastery of each. Don't lie to yourself about being current; you can fool everybody but the airplane.

Part VI
Your Own Airplane

Chapter 32
First Love

Well, well, so you've finally gone and made a deal to buy an airplane after months of scanning the want ads, bugging airplane dealers, and hanging around airports. Oh, maybe it's not exactly brand new, but it's just what you've always wanted, and it's something you've been working toward for a long, long, time. Congratulations; I hope you'll both be very happy.

But before you rush back home to drain your bank account, and forthwith return to take possession of this beauty, are you *really* sure you know what you're getting into? Oh, you do, huh? You say you had Joe the mechanic look the bird over and check its logbooks, just like you read about. Good, good; now what about insurance, the registration and radio license forms, and all the other stuff? You hadn't gotten around to those details, eh? Welcome to the ranks of aircraft owners, good buddy; you've got a lot to learn.

The Paperwork

First, taking delivery of your new property involves a little paperwork, and some common sense as well. Your friend, Joe the mechanic, has seen that the required papers—such as the Airworthiness certificate, weight and balance data, operating limitations and logbooks—were all in order. Now, as the purchaser, you need to get the previous owner to sign a proper bill of sale, such as (but not necessarily) the FAA's AC form 8050-2. Remember, if the aircraft was registered to a partnership, all partners must sign the bill of sale, even if you're only buying one partner's interest in the aircraft. No notarization is required.

You will apply for a certificate of registration on AC form 8050-1, which must be sent with the bill of sale to the FAA Aircraft Registry in Oklahoma City, Oklahoma; the fee as of this writing is

$5.00. The pink copy of the application is to be carried in the aircraft as temporary registration, valid for 90 days, pending receipt of your new registration.

It is important to realize that the FAA does not guarantee ownership; in other words, a registration certificate is not a "clear title" per se. Liens may be outstanding against the aircraft despite the apparent ownership conveyed by proper registration. Lien holders can register their liens with the FAA for another $5.00 fee, and before you purchase any aircraft it would be wise to have the FAA files searched for outstanding liens, a service performed not by the FAA but by private title search firms located in Oklahoma City. Such a search would be money well spent unless you are quite sure of the bird's history. There could, of course, be unrecorded liens not filed in the FAA registry.

Next, since there is a radio transmitter or two on board most airplanes, a change of ownership calls for a new application for a radio station license on FCC form 404. This form goes to the Federal Communications Commission in Gettysburg, Pennsylvania; no fee is being charged at this time. While you're waiting for your new license, the old license will serve for up to 90 days. When applying for the license, check any categories of transmitter you may be adding to the airplane in the future, such as a DME or radar altimeter, so you will not have to reapply later. The Aircraft Radio Station license is valid for five years.

Local Taxes and Registration

If you live in a state that features state registration of aircraft, don't forget to 'fess up to the local boys; they expect their tribute, usually on an annual basis. More importantly, check out the applicability of sales tax laws, both in the state of purchase and your own state, if different. Those sales tax investigators get pretty sharp about tracking down violators on big-ticket items like aircraft, and you don't want to get hit with a large penalty-laden bill later on. It'll only cost more then, so you may as well pay up now.

Insure Thyself

It would be wise to avail yourself of some insurance coverage before you go winging away. Other owners can refer you to brokers or companies handling their insurance. The broker will need to know the airplane's identifying numbers and your qualifications in order to bind the coverage. This can be arranged before you go to take delivery, so you need not risk an uninsured trip.

While there is no federal law requiring you to carry any insurance at all, it would be pretty dumb not to have liability protection, at the very least. It's a hungry world out there, and people get sued by their friends every day. If you should inadvertently get involved in a mishap that kills or injures a passenger or an innocent bystander on the ground, you will need coverage. Protection against windstorm and other ground damage losses may cost relatively little additional premium. Also, at least some of the more-expensive inflight hull coverage may be needed to protect your banker's interest, if you have the airplane financed.

The Checkout

After seeing to the insurance, what about getting a checkout? If you're already experienced in that type of aircraft, you may feel qualified in the airplane after only a few minutes in the cockpit with the previous owner. Just make sure he tells you about all the knobs that don't work and the switches that don't switch. More than likely, however, you will need a qualified CFI to ride with you, one who is familiar with this make and model of airplane. A CFI checkout may also be a requirement of your insurance policy, without which you aren't covered.

If you are buying a high-performance airplane (over 200 horsepower, or with flaps, retractable gear, and a controllable propeller) you must have a certification of competence to fly such an airplane in your logbook, unless you logged time in some type of high-performance airplane before November 1, 1973. Be sure to mention this to the instructor who gives you your checkout, or he may not sign you off properly.

Staying Legal

Any required ADs (Airworthiness Directives) to be performed on your airplane will be mailed to the previous owner until the paperwork changing the registration clears Oklahoma City, so ask him to forward such vital mailings. In case of multiple ownership, the first owner listed gets the mail. If a transponder is on board, make sure it's legal for use as required by FAR 91.177; whether VFR or IFR, it must be inspected by a repair station each 24 months. If you plan to fly instruments, you will need to check the logbooks for an altimeter/static system test within the past two years, and, of course, verify and sign off the VOR receivers as being within tolerance.

As you can see, owning your own bird means a lot of details suddenly become *your* responsibility. When an annual inspection is due, it's your obligation to see that it's scheduled, not the mechanic's. When an AD is issued on your make and model, you are responsible for having it complied with, and are to maintain a record of such compliances. It would be well to have a little extra cash laid back for unexpected maintenance bills. In our enthusiasm, we often underestimate the cost of keeping an airplane, particularly an older, complex one such as a Bonanza or Cessna 182.

But there is a lot of satisfaction is pulling those keys out of your pocket and saying, "That's my airplane, I can go fly anytime I want; I don't have to wait in line or ask anybody's permission." Enjoy your new pride and joy, first-time owner!

Chapter 33

Making a Checklist

To many pilots, being able to fire up and take off without the aid of a printed checklist is living proof of their maturity. For them, it is an admission of weakness to resort to any sort of memory aid. While it is true that your personal airplane eventually becomes so familiar that you seem to know standard procedures by heart, such familiarity can be a long time coming, and even then the stress of an unusual situation can make you forget. A simple list of things to be checked before, during, and after a flight can prevent many an interesting moment, and perhaps save a bent airplane.

Some need the checklist for other reasons. Rental pilots, as well as those owning an airplane in partnership, have to contend with another person's habits and fallibilities. If the last pilot turned the fuel valve off when parking, contrary to your habits, and you make a hasty departure without checking it, the engine could sputter to a halt at just the wrong moment. Were all radios left on by the previous pilot, ready to be injured by your start-up? Perhaps a fuse or light bulb burned out on the last trip, and you are the next person to fly the unrepaired ship. By all means, if you share an airplane, have *and use* a checklist.

Check the Airplane, Not the List

One word of caution regarding the use of a checklist, however: *Do not place blind faith in a simple celluloid card.* Familiarity can lead you to look at the list without actually reading it, and you may speed down the card, confident that you checked over the list, all the while skipping one or more items. You, as the pilot, are to check out the airplane, not the checklist. Move your finger or thumb down the page one line at a time, and touch or move the item checked with the other hand, using physical contact to confirm the check.

In general, checklists provided by the aircraft manufacturers are next to useless. The ones printed on the instrument panel or sidewall are too brief, and the lists contained in the pilot's handbook are awkward to locate and handle. The best checklists are still those on a single piece of durable card stock small enough to fit the hand comfortably and big enough to be found easily among the litter in the map pockets or glove compartment. A 5×8-inch card is about right, although I prefer a slimmer 4×9-inch card, easily obtained by whacking a strip out of a file folder.

Don't acquire a new airplane and immediately type up a detailed checklist for it. You will wind up wishing you had included extra items or arranged them in different order. It's best to rough out a preliminary list, use it for several hours of flying, and make revisions to it until it fits your exact needs. You may not want a direct copy of someone else's checklist; every pilot has his or her special concerns or faults to be checked against. However, basic lists can be expanded to fit nearly any aircraft or pilot.

Arranging the List

Divide the checklist into sections, which makes it easier to find where you should resume checking, by creating convenient "quittin' places." A "Before Entering Aircraft" section might include switches off, fuel on, controls unlocked, preflight inspection okay, weight and balance checked, and so on. The next division, "Before Starting Engine," should be a logical sequence to check basic items and get the fire lit. "Seat Belts and Harness Fastened" is an item required by regulation, "Doors Shut and Latched" saves surprises later, and "Baggage Secure" keeps loose objects out of unwanted places. Brake pedals should be squeezed to test for an empty master cylinder. Controls should be checked for full, free, and correct travel. Fuel value is confirmed "On," all electrical and radio switches "Off," followed by normal starting procedure. This section should conclude with a few items to be noted after the engine is started, such as oil pressure coming up, primer locked and radios "On."

You should now be ready to leave the ramp, letting the engine come up to operating temperature while enroute to the runup area. When reaching the runup position, resume at the next section, headed "Before Takeoff." Again, controls should be checked, in case you picked up a cornstalk or something while enroute to the pad, or just plain fired up without the checklist. Trim settings are important, and flaps should be cycled, whether manual or electric, to see if they work normally and at the same time. I like to spell out the setting of directional gyro and altimeter in specific items, but generally lump the scan of other gauges under "Check Instruments for Normal Indication."

Leaving the actual runup until near the end of the pre-takeoff section gives the engine a few more seconds to warm up before winding it up to the specified rpm for checking mags, carb heat, prop, and vacuum, as applicable to your bird. Limits of mag drop and other parameters should be on the card; in case you get curious about an indication it saves digging out the manual. You may wish to include a mag grounding check at idle rpm at this point, or perhaps at the shutdown location on the list. It is well to include another check of the doors' security, since they may have been propped open during taxi for ventilation.

I like to conclude the pre-takeoff list with a recheck of the fuel selector on the correct position, and a reminder to look for other traffic before taking the runway. You may have all sorts of extra items you want added for your airplane's list, so go right ahead; that's why you're making a list—to keep you or a friend who flies the airplane occasionally from letting something important slip by.

In the Air

Inflight portions of the checklist should be kept brief, since the user will be busy with other duties and shouldn't be looking down at his lap too much. Best climb speeds and EGT-leaning parameters would be helpful reminders, and commonly used cruise-power settings can be included. The "Before Landing" list will include let-down items that may have been overlooked, such as mixture rich, cowl flaps open (or closed, as desired), and main tanks or boost pump selection. A gear-down item should be included early in the "Before Landing" section, and once again at its conclusion, to make sure a safe indication resulted from moving the gear handle. Gear and flap limit speeds should be on the list to help unfamiliar pilots who may miss the placards.

The "After Landing" items will include such reminders as carburetor heat off, cowl flaps open, flaps up, boost pump off, strobes extinguished, and transponder recycled to standby. The last section, "Shutdown Procedure," should restore all electrical and radio switches to "Off" before the mixture knob is pulled; I find it convenient to follow an L-shaped path down the avionics stack to the mixture knob, then across the electric switches as the engine dies. The key should be removed from the magneto switch as a double-check that the switch is off, and the control lock should be installed. The final item should be "Secure Aircraft," a reminder to either tie down or hangar the bird before leaving it.

After revising your list into its final form, prepare to type your checklist on good heavy card stock that will still feed through a typewriter, such as 90-pound index card or 11-point manila file folder. Use a fresh typewriter ribbon so you will be able to read the list even in poor light. I like to have the entire pre-takeoff list on one side of the card, so there is no need to flip over to finish. Keep the wording simple, so use of the checklist will require a minimum of skill or deduction by unfamiliar hands (Tables 33-1, 33-2).

Preserving Your Handiwork

To protect the checklist some sort of clear overlay should be

Table 33-1. Sample Checklist for Cessna 182B Skylane, Front.

BEFORE ENTERING AIRCRAFT	BEFORE TAKEOFF
1. Remove controls lock 2. Confirm ignition off 3. Check fuel selector "Both" 4. Perform preflight inspection	1. Brakes set 2. Controls free and correct 3. Trim tabs set for takeoff 4. Altimeter set for field elev. 5. Directional gyro set 6. Instruments checked (green arcs)
BEFORE STARTING ENGINE	7. Fuel adequate for flight, "Both On"
1. Weight and balance checked 2. Safety belts fastened 3. Doors closed and locked 4. Controls unlocked and free 5. Brakes set	8. RUN-UP - 1700 rpm Magnetos; max drop 125 rpm Propeller; drop in rpm Carburetor heat; drop in rpm Vacuum gauge; 4.6 to 5.4 Hg 9. Acceleration test 10. Flaps as required
STARTING PROCEDURE	11. Recheck; prop in, carb heat cold, cowl flaps open
1. Fuel selector "Both" 2. Mixture full rich 3. Carburetor heat cold 4. Cowl flaps open 5. Propeller high-rpm 6. Radios, lights, etc. off 7. Master switch on 8. Throttle cracked ½-inch 9. Prime as required 10. Propeller area CLEAR 11. Magneto switch "Both" 12. Engage starter 13. Check oil pressure 14. Avionics "On" as required 15. Idle 800 rpm for warm-up	12. Autopilot off 13. Anticollision lights on 14. Transponder on 15. Clearance if required 16. Check for traffic before takeoff CLIMB 1. Best rate 88 mph, best angle 70 mph 2. Cruise-climb power, 23" & 2450 rpm 3. Cowl flaps open as required

CRUISE

1. Cowl flaps closed
2. Normal cruise-22" & 2300 rpm
3. Lean 100° rich of peak EGT

BEFORE LANDING

1. Mixture full rich
2. Fuel selector "Both"
3. Carburetor heat checked, on if required
4. 12" m.p. for approach
5. Trim as required for 90 mph glide
6. Autopilot off
7. Flaps as required (100 mph maximum)
8. Propeller full in on short final
9. Normal approach 80 mph, short-field 70 mph

AFTER LANDING

1. Raise flaps after rollout
2. Carburetor heat cold
3. Cowl flaps open
4. Transponder & strobes off

SHUTDOWN PROCEDURE

1. Check for ELT signals (121.5)
2. Engine idle
3. Radios off
4. Mixture full lean
5. Electrical switches off
6. Magnetos off, key out
7. Master switch off
8. Fuel selector "Off"
9. Controls lock installed
10. Secure aircraft

used. A plastic envelope of the correct size would allow the list to be removed and updated, or you may prefer to laminate your efforts in plastic. The lamination adds stiffness as well as sealing out grime; the sticky-back acetate sheets are available at most stationery stores. Cut the sheet a half-inch larger than your checklist to give a margin for sloppy placement. Peel off the backing and lay a sheet down sticky side up. Starting at one end, place the checklist on top of it, smoothing it down onto the laminating sheet gradually to keep air bubbles to a minimum. Small bubbles can be worked out by rubbing the surface with a blunt instrument. Get the card lined up right the first time, because there's no moving it once it makes contact! After both sides have been coated, trim the sealed edges of the plastic, leaving a quarter-inch or so of overlap to prevent delamination.

Put your name and aircraft number on the checklist, because if you do a good job on its preparation it might be borrowed by someone who admires your work, never to return. Use the checklist, and you'll find it saving you time as well as bringing order to your checkout of the airplane. It's just a simple reminder, but the times when you're in the biggest hurry are when you are most likely to skip a vital item.

Chapter 34

Test Flying Your Airplane

Most pilots will eventually encounter an airplane that has been taken apart and put back together again. While it may not be officially required by regulation, any airplane that is fresh out of the shop must be given a test flight of some sort. It may be the first flight after a hundred-hour inspection or annual, or it could be the aftermath of a major rebuilding job. Whatever the cause, if you're going to be the lucky person who gets to make such a flight, you should know how to go about it safely.

Test flying needn't mean a death-defying adventure with a parachute strapped on and crash trucks standing by; that's for *experimental* test flying, where the pilot is a flying engineer probing unexplored areas of a design's limitations. In most cases, the owner/pilot will be flying a tried-and-proven machine with only a little extra care needed to assure that all is well before returning it to full duty. However, it would be particularly wise to avoid night or IFR flight if you're picking an airplane up fresh from the shop, until it has been shaken down. If the task is somewhat experimental, such as when making the first flight of a rebuilt or a new homebuilt aircraft, don't be ashamed to seek a professional pilot, rather than flying it yourself if you're short on experience; there's no sense risking all that hard work.

The Simple Return-to-Service Check

Let's start with some of the more commonplace tasks—for instance, flying an airplane that has been given an annual inspection or thorough hundred-hour. In theory, such an airplane shouldn't need any extra care at all, since it has just been signed off as airworthy. People are human, though, and people make mistakes; some people are just more human than others. I have had shimmy-dampeners left dangling, fuel caps left off, oil screens only finger-tight, and lots of other good things, all under the guise of routine maintenance. Of course, you're not going to trust your airplane to a shop you don't feel sure of, but the FARs make it quite clear: The final responsibility for making sure an airplane is ready for flight rests with the pilot who is making that flight. So check everything, no matter *who* says it's ready to go.

If possible, spend some time in the shop along with the airplane, if you can manage not to make a nuisance of yourself. Wear old clothes, stay out of the way, and offer to handle screwdriver jobs like removing fairings or inspection covers. Look your airplane over while it's opened up; it's amazing how many things can happen inside over a year's time, and the more eyes that are in there looking, the more things will be caught instead of missed. The engine compartment requires about half the work of a lightplane inspection, so keep an eye out for chafing controls or cracked, worn, or loose items. Add anything found to the squawk list brought in with the airplane so it will come to the A&P's attention; don't interrupt his work every few minutes with trivia, or you'll have a very expensive inspection!

Keep a mental note of any repairs or alterations that could affect the coming flight, such as removal of control surfaces or partial teardown of the engine or accessories. Knowing what items have been repaired will give you a chance to monitor them closely for an unhealthy sign after takeoff. As the reassembly progresses, begin your preflight inspection; watch for wrenches hiding between cylinder heads, cowling screws not tightened, hubcaps left off, or battery cables disconnected.

If you are picking up an airplane that has been left at the shop, find the mechanic who did the work and learn what was done; don't depend on the itemized bill you picked up at the front office. The A&P may even want to ride with you to check the results of adjustments he made. In any event, preflight the bird with a fine-tooth comb, as if you've never seen it before. Visually check fuel and oil levels, control freedom, and the general security of fittings and covers.

Before starting the engine, check for full, unrestricted travel of throttle, propeller, mixture, carburetor heat, and cowl-flap controls, and see that flight controls move correctly in response to your wishes; aileron travel should be checked with the elevators in full up and full down positions. Start the engine, monitoring pressure and temperature indications, and warm up no more than necessary for smooth acceleration to taxi power. Check the brakes as you begin to

158

Fig. 34-1. When an airplane leaves the shop, it should be gone over with a fine-tooth comb. Never assume that a mechanic or his helper can't make a mistake.

roll, before you get close to other aircraft or buildings; there should be even braking with no fade or odd noises. Check nosewheel or tailwheel steering during taxi, and park into the wind for the runup, particularly if the engine has been overhauled and is still "tight."

Check all engine instruments for normal readings; the fuel gauges should agree with your visual findings, and careful ignition and propeller-cycle tests made at the recommended rpm. If you believe a full-throttle runup is justified, keep it as short as possible and make sure you're not blasting people or property behind you. In most cases, you could determine the engine's full-throttle output at the start of the takeoff roll with plenty of room to stop.

As you make a normal takeoff and climbout, remain in the traffic pattern to gain altitude and note the aircraft's performance. By doing so you will be close to a landing spot if something suddenly goes wrong, rather than several miles away from the strip. Follow the shop's instructions about power settings and climb speeds with a newly reworked engine; by ready to increase climb speed or level off if overheating occurs. In most cases an airplane that has undergone no more than a routine inspection will exhibit few unusual traits, but be listening for new sounds or vibrations if you are familiar with the airplane's normal characteristics. I'll never forget the screws that were left untightened in an aileron inspection cover, falling out in

159

short order until only one screw remained to hold the cover broadside to the wind; it took a half-deflection of the control wheel to maintain level flight until we got back on the ground. If you hear a new buzz or thump, land and check it out before you leave the area.

Test-Hopping a New or Rebuilt Airplane

When flying an airplane that has been rebuilt after extensive damage, or a spanking new homebuilt, even more attention to preflight details is called for. Wait until winds favor the longest runway available, and do a little study of the forced-landing areas available nearby. If runway length permits, a partial takeoff will allow a sampling of control response just above the runway, followed by a landing straight ahead. Most standard designs are predictable if factory rigging is followed, thus producing few surprises for the test pilot.

In the eventual takeoff, allow the airplane to lift itself off well above stall speed to assure good control and check the takeoff trim setting for correctness as you accelerate into a climb. Waste no time getting to altitude, since this is your best insurance in any emergency, and avoid built-up areas and housing as much as possible. Make no power reductions until a healthy margin of altitude is gained.

If no unusual tendencies present themselves, continue a cruising climb to at least 3000 feet AGL and level out to check rigging and stability. Trim should be adequate to allow hands-off flight in smooth air; observe any deviations from straight flight for ground adjustment later. If a turn consistently begins after the controls are released, is it the result of drag from a yaw of the nose or a true "heavy wing" that goes down before the heading changes? Which is needed to keep the skid/slip ball centered in straight-and-level flight, aileron or rudder? Bringing back such facts will tell the mechanic where to change rigging or add trim correction.

A correctly loaded airplane trimmed for cruise should recover hands-off promptly from a smooth pull-up to a speed 20 percent below cruise, by oscillating into diminishing climbs and dives until once again in level flight. Any prolonged climb or dive indicates poor CG placement or inadequate stabilizer area. Slight yaws induced with rudder application should snap back to straight flight when the pedal is released. However, most aircraft will stabilize into a spiral if a wing is permitted to stay down after displacement from level flight. A slow-flight check will sample control at near-landing speed and the amount of P-factor generated in a go-around.

160

Stalls should be conducted to calibrate the airspeed indicator before landing, by slowing at a rate of one mph per second in landing configuration until a definite stall occurs. A figure 1.6 times this speed should be maintained for safe maneuvering in a glide, and 1.4 times the stall speed used for final approach. If the stall occurred at 50 mph, 80 mph would be a safe traffic pattern speed and 70 mph a good approach speed for the first attempt. Any consistent wing drop at the stall break should be noted, but make sure you aren't inducing it by uncoordinated use of rudder during the entry.

Operate all equipment and controls during the flight, checking fuel feed from various tanks, electrical load carried as radios and lights are turned on, and all flight instruments for normal readings. Pull on the cabin heater to check for exhaust smell as well as heat output; a freshpaint odor would be normal with a new engine, and a solvent aroma is to be expected if the engine has just been washed down.

If an engine is being broken in, make the traffic pattern under power to avoid excessive sudden cooling. A near-stalling touchdown should allow stopping without riding the brakes, although their stopping power should be tested briefly. Cool the engine down by a few minutes of idle or slow taxiing, and check that idle speed does not exceed 550-600 rpm with the throttle full back. Moving the mixture to idle-cutoff should produce an increase of 25 to 50 rpm before the engine dies, if the carburetor or fuel control is properly adjusted.

When you pick up an airplane from the shop, don't just ask if it's ready to go; before you blast off for home, spend a few minutes checking it out, no matter what anyone says. Be mentally prepared to be a test pilot for that first hour or so. The next hour might not be so convenient.

Chapter 35

When You Bend Your Bird

It happens: Despite all your precautions and every last-ditch effort to prevent it, your turn comes; you have an accident, you break an airplane. Accidents may always happen to the other guy, but suddenly you've become the other guy.

When the crunch comes, your first priority is always preservation of life and limb. We can replace airplanes, but when people are killed or hurt they can never be made whole again, as if it had never happened. After the crash trucks are gone and the dust settles, the brief paragraphs of National Transportation Safety Board Regulation Part 830 take on a new significance. There are procedures to be followed and regulations to be satisfied.

What's an Accident?

What constitutes an accident, anyway? Contrary to popular opinion, it is not based on a dollar estimate or a personal injury index. Rather, the National Transportation Safety Board calls an aircraft mishap an accident, for reporting purposes, when substantial damage is done to the aircraft, or serious injury occurs to a person resulting from the aircraft's operation. *Serious injury* means immediate or subsequent hopitalization for injuries suffered in the accident. A fatality, of course, always makes it a reportable accident, even if the aircraft is not damaged.

Substantial damage would be any damage rendering the aircraft unairworthy, such as bent wing structure, crumpled fuselage, broken tail surfaces, or a damaged firewall. Non-reportable damage would be that which is limited to the engine, propeller, a control surface, or other component.

Therefore, you can have a connecting rod failure, land in a rock-strewn pasture where you blow out a tire and puncture the fuselage fabric, and hit your nose on the panel hard enough to make it bleed profusely, and you still have not had an accident, by the terms of the NTSB regulations. Yet if you veer off the runway and run into a hangar, striking the airplane's wingtip hard enough to wrinkle the wing spar, it would have to be termed significant damage and reported.

Notification, Reporting, and Preservation

The time interval for reporting an accident is often misunderstood as being 10 days or 72 hours; actually, the NTSB must be notified *immediately*, either directly or through an FAA district office. This initial phone call is usually followed by a written report on an NTSB form, which is due in 10 days. If you're unfortunate enough to be involved in an accident, there are certain basic procedures that should be followed. The owner of the aircraft should be notified at once, of course, if not on the scene.

Enlist aid to secure the accident site from scavengers; the general public has a ghoulish fascination for wrecks and will drive for miles just for the chance to pick up souvenirs, important pieces that could be the only clue to the accident's cause. Even if they leave empty-handed, their footprints can track up skid marks and impact areas important to the investigation. Law enforcement officials are generally familiar with the site-preservation aspect of investigation, so call the gendarmes at once. When working with a wreck be alert

Fig. 35-1. All occupants safely escaped from this wrecked Skyhawk; now the paperwork and legal maneuverings begin.

for hazards, such as broken glass or plastic, open accumulations of fuel, and torn sheet metal. If it is necessary to move any part of the wreckage for safety reasons, or to change the position of a valve or control, mark the object carefully to guide the investigation team.

The more serious the accident, the more involved the investigation becomes. If no injuries result, and the circumstances were clear-cut, an investigation might not be made at all and the entire matter may be handled over the phone or by mail. But if injuries or fatalities occur, an NTSB team or the FAA personnel will be dispatched to the scene, with the FAA usually handling the less serious, non air-carrier accidents.

Remember, do not move the wreckage until cleared to do so by the investigating authority. It would be wise to shoot some pictures of the scene in case questions arise later. As soon as possible, the wreckage should be moved to an out-of-sight area to lessen the crowd attractions. A locked hangar is best; failing this, a sheltered spot out of sight of the general public should be used. The pile of debris may be sitting for some weeks before a final insurance settlement and disposition is made, so plan accordingly.

Insurance

The aircraft owner would want to notify his insurance underwriters as soon as possible and, if the pilot is not the owner, he will soon learn about the coverage he didn't have. A rented or borrowed aircraft is not necessarily covered against mishaps while in the hands of a non-owner pilot and, even if covered, subrogation may be undertaken to recover damages from the pilot. For this reason, the pilot should make no statements that could be taken as an admission of liability unless he understands the consequences. On the other hand, it is helpful to write down what occurred as soon as possible to prevent forgetting some vital detail which could help explain the sequence of events.

Forms will be forthcoming—in quantity. Make copies of everything for your own files. The NTSB will want form 6120.1 completed within 10 days; it simply lists the circumstances of the accident and gives a statistical breakout of the pilot's qualifications and experience. The insurance company will have a similar form, parts of which may require completion by both the pilot and the owner, if different. If it appears that the pilot may have precipitated the accident by poor flying technique, the FAA can issue a request that the pilot take some dual instruction in the areas deemed deficient, such as crosswind landings, fuel management, instrument procedures, etc. This form is to be signed off by an instructor after the required dual is completed, although a further flight check by an FAA inspector may be needed to return the pilot to flight status.

Every accident should be treated as a learning opportunity. Bad as they are, they can serve a purpose in educating the pilot involved and all others on the scene. Unfortunately, experience is a very expensive method of learning and we must strive to prevent each mishap from occurring, to hold down our insurance rates and present a more positive image to the general public. But if an accident does happen, make the best of the situation and learn something from it.

Part VII
Going On

Chapter 36
Flight Review Due?

It will usually happen about once a week. A fellow airman will seek me out to ask in a quavering voice, "How rough are you gonna be on my flight review?" As a flight instructor, empowered by the eternal and the FAA to make a pilot airworthy with one stroke of a pen, I am expected to be a cross between a fire-breathing dragon and a father-confessor. Shucks, fellas, I was drafted into this outfit just like you were; I'm as anxious as anybody to make it through without complications.

The flight review is like a misbegotten relative nobody wants to claim. Its origin and early childhood weren't widely discussed, and because fiction often makes more enjoyable conversation than fact, the reputation of the flight review remains besmirched. Like the sailor's tattoo of a green alligator, the flight review seemed to be a good idea at the time. But when the proposal to require an instructor's evaluation every 24 months was cast into a regulation in 1973, nobody knew what to expect. The instructors weren't told much other than to look for proficiency commensurate with the ratings held, and the pilots were simply told to get an instructor's signature in their logbooks or quit flying. With this lack of guidelines, pilots didn't know what to prepare for and instructors didn't know how to conduct the ride, and the first round of flight reviews varied widely in content and complexity. Fortunately, industry and government got together after a year or so and devised some nonregulatory guidelines to help straighten out the mess, but the bad taste from the initial poor start is with us still.

The lack of enthusiasm for flight reviews also probably stems from their manner of promulgation. They were more or less demanded by the National Transportation Safety Board as a way of reducing pilot-error accidents, and everybody consulted agreed that it sounded like a good idea. But the FAA only wrote the basic law, at NTSB's behest, leaving the rest up to nature. Meanwhile, pilots felt they were doing quite all right, thank you, and suddenly here was another rule thrust upon them against their wishes. "Here, take it, it's good for you." Blah! You get the idea. To get cooperation, you must first convince the patient he's sick.

Make the Best of It

It behooves you to make the best of the situation; as long as you have to have a flight review anyway, make it something productive. Ideally, a pilot could get a new rating of some sort every two years and save the need for a flight review altogether, because any flight check takes the place of the review. But most people aren't interested in collecting ratings, and even so there is a limit to the ratings one can afford to acquire. Short of pursuing a new rating, one could schedule a good round of dual instruction and avail himself of some instrument refresher work, aerobatic dual, mountain experience, or whatever.

So maybe you're not crazy about the idea of baring your soul to an instructor after two years of freedom? Perhaps you're afraid he or she will uncover some hidden flaw that'll wound your pride? Or are you just "too busy?" Whatever your reason for avoiding the flight review, *don't*. Sure, nobody's likely to check you, especially if you're only flying your own airplane. But if you should have the misfortune to be involved in an accident while operating without a valid endorsement, you're going to be in a heap of trouble. Oh, you can bluff your way past the FAA; about all they can do is revoke or suspend your license. But when your insurance company finds you were in violation of the FARs, you could get hurt in the old pocketbook because they may just refuse to settle your claim. So if you aren't going to take a flight review, you may just as well cancel your insurance and save the premium money.

Fear not; there is surely an instructor somewhere you can take into your confidence, swear to secrecy, and fly with long enough to prove your prowess. Looking at it another way, if you're good enough to "pass" the review, what are you worrying about? And if you really are doubtful about your chances of being good enough, you *need* the review. I can tell you that some sort of recurrent training is needed, though. We've always preached that, but only the Flying Farmers ever believed in it strongly enough to make it a requirement as part of their discount insurance coverage. So we got the flight review as a result of our intransigence.

It's amazing how many nervous pilots I ride with on flight reviews. Even if I tell them they're going to pass unless they scare me, they still sweat out the ride with me, a harmless old "fright" instructor. I couldn't bust anybody if I wanted to. About all I can do is hit the ground running after the ride and refuse to sign your logbook, if you're really *that* dangerous. So get your favorite CFI to tell you what to expect and find out how you stack up.

Some Typical Problems

As an example of the lack of self-initiated practice, consider the discussions I get into about stalls. I have ridden with numerous pilots who haven't stalled their airplane since the last flight review. A couple of stalls every two years is no way to maintain your mastery over the machinery, friends, and it shows. If your airplane is so dangerous that you're afraid to practice some stalls at altitude every month or so, you shouldn't by flying it. By the same token, if your proficiency is so lacking that you don't trust yourself to do a simple stall, what makes you think you're sharp enough to make a good crosswind landing or a short-field takeoff?

Another sore nerve I frequently touch during a flight review is the forced landing. Lots of pilots haven't heard the prop windmilling since their primary training days; every landing they make requires a lengthy, power-boosted approach, aimed at a mile-long ribbon of concrete. They have no idea of their airplane's sink rate or glide ratio with the power off because they haven't practiced a forced landing since they flew a light trainer. I can give you the names of a few pilots who are darned glad they had practiced their engine-out technique; the ability to execute a forced landing saved their bacon when the fan suddenly stopped one day. Unfortunately, I can also count a couple of friends who aren't around anymore because they weren't up to handling a sudden power failure. So don't wait for the flight review to come around to shoot a landing with the engine at idle; give it a try periodically.

Know thy airplane. This is a basic tenet of flying we often overlook, a fact that usually shows up on the flight review. What is your airplane's best angle of climb airspeed? You really ought to know in case you need to use it someday. What's your bird's useful load? Don't give me that old saw about "She'll carry anything you can shut the door on;" if I hear that one again I'll choke. I want the flight review applicant to know the airplane's numbers, the basic data every pilot should have down cold before he takes the airplane up. Yet I have reviewed pilots who have owned their airplane for years without learning the operating details. If you can't tell me how to safely jump-start your airplane, or what your fuel system's weaknesses are, or what your rpm and manifold pressure gauges should be reading as you roll for takeoff, you're going to know before we part.

Be Choosy

Don't ride with just anybody who happens to possess an instructor's certificate. Find an instructor whom you feel can teach you something and get some good out of fulfilling an obligation. If you're an instrument pilot, find a practicing CFI-I to give you the review. If you fly multi-engine airplanes, you need a many-motor instructor beside you on the flight review. If you are a glider-guider, hunt up an FIG for assistance. If you're an ATP type, get a fellow graybeard to ride with you. If you're an antiquer, homebuilder, or warbird freak, ride with one of your own kind. Don't waste your time with an instructor who can't relate to your type of flying.

All instructors—myself included—occasionally forget what we're about on the review ride. The flight review is not a period of dual, it's an evaluation of a pilot's knowledge and ability. The dual can come later, if needed or requested, and we instructors should try to avoid giving lectures or demonstrations during the flight review. I am not supposed to remake every pilot into my image of the perfect aviator; my job is just to see if the specimen sitting beside me exhibits any deviate tendencies that could bring him to grief if not corrected. As long as the flying mistakes and blank responses are minor enough to be covered with practice and study, the flight review can be signed off with a little dual recommended. If *el piloto* is just an accident going somewhere to happen, however, the dual will be required before I can sign him off.

The success of the flight review concept depends utterly on the general public's response to it. Treat it as an opportunity, make it work for you, and you'll benefit from it. Ignore it as needless harrassment, and you'll eventually prove the need for just such a requirement. The choice is yours.

Chapter 37

Want to Learn Aerobatics?

Joining the ranks of aerobatic pilots is an excellent way to expand your flying horizons beyond basic Point-A-to-Point-B aviating. At this time there is no pilot rating for aerobatic flight; if you would like to try upside-down flying, the way you go about it is up to you. Unfortunately, many pilots attempt aerobatic maneuvers without fully understanding the dangers involved. It looked so easy when the airshow pilot did that loop or barrel roll, yet one must realize there is a fine line drawn between safety and disaster for the unknowledgeable pilot.

Airplanes aren't made of boilerplate; they are built only as strong as necessary to meet certain standards of certification. Otherwise, they would have almost no payload and would be of little practical use. Naturally, an aerobatic airplane must be designed with excess structural strength, as well as having superb control ability, in order to withstand the stresses of a maneuver that doesn't work out as planned. In addition, a good aerobatic ship is also inherently a little unstable—not always a desirable characteristic in everyday flying.

Don't Overstress Yourself

As an example of the dangers involved in simple aerobatics, it is possible to fly an aileron roll within a maximum G loading of 1½ to 2 Gs, well below the stress limits of even normal and utility category airplanes. Yet if the pilot errs slightly in nose position as the airplane goes inverted, the maneuver can turn into a sloppy rolling split-S, and more than four Gs easily can be pulled in the resulting recovery. Throw in a little rough air, or panicky control handling, and the airplane could be severely damaged from overstress.

True, a utility category airplane has a 50 percent overload

factor, beyond its design load factor of 4.4 positive Gs, making the ultimate yield point 6.6 Gs, but this was for a factory-new, unfatigued, uncorroded airframe. Also, to exceed the design load factor even slightly can still result in permanent deformation of the structure, even though nothing actually falls apart. The partial failure then lies in wait for the next pilot, who could get into some rough air in the course of a normal flight and experience structural failure, all because somebody had tried to prove their prowess as a hot-rock aerobatic pilot.

How to Learn Aerobatics the Right Way . . .

As in all flying, there is a right way and a wrong way to learn about aerobatics. The right way is to use a tested, proven airplane designed for aerobatics with the guidance of an experienced aerobatic pilot; if he or she is a CFI, so much the better. Bear in mind that even aerobatic certificated airplanes have their limitations, and can't be tossed about in any maneuver you choose at any entry speed you like.

Pilots interested in trying out new maneuvers or procedures will wear parachutes and seek high altitudes over unpopulated areas for their experimentation; that's one reason cabin-type aerobatic machines are equipped with quick-jettison doors. Only when operating within the certificated limitations of the airplane can a reasonable level of safety be achieved; if the book doesn't show approval for outside loops, don't try 'em!

A G-meter should be on board, both as a warning against high stresses and as an aid to precision flying. You cannot always feel G-loading well enough to stay within limits, especially as tolerance to aerobatics is acquired. However, aerobatic novices will probably not watch the accelerometer or airspeed indicator during their first snap rolls or spins—they're doing well just to stay oriented! A shoulder harness—or even better, a five-strap restraint system with a backup safety belt— is vital to hold you firmly in your seat during all attitudes.

Again I stress, *don't try to teach yourself aerobatics from scratch,* no matter how easy it looked when you saw it done, or how simple it sounded when described. Get some time with an experienced, knowledgeable pilot; there is no substitute for hands-on flying through a maneuver with a skilled person at your side.

. . . And the Wrong Way

Most importantly, don't use a stock airplane for aerobatics. A standard 152 is a different bird from a 152 Aerobat, and it simply isn't strong enough to withstand the possible G-load resulting from mistakes. Sure, you've seen some pretty flashy aerobatic routines performed in stock airplanes at airshows, but these were being done by a pilot who had learned aerobatics first in a beefy airplane, and who flew the stock airplane very carefully to avoid exceeding its lower stress limits. We all know a Strike Commander can do slow rolls and loops; the trick is to do them safely, within limits, and without getting into a low-level trap with no escape.

You might have heard that older airplanes, such as Luscombes or Taylorcrafts, are okay for aerobatic training, since they do not have "aerobatics prohibited" in their limitations and "they built 'em tough back then." Yes and no; these old birds were licensed without specific limitations on specific maneuvers, leaving it up to the pilot to decide what to attempt. Today's airplanes are certificated only for specific maneuvers at certain maximum entry speeds, giving the pilot more guidance with which to stay out of trouble. In any event, bear in mind that a 35-year-old airplane may have brittle bones; the structure should be closely watched and G-loads kept light.

A good aerobatic flight is not a wild dogfight in the sky, tumbling through one maneuver into another helter-skelter. Planning is needed to ensure that available altitude is expended wisely, and that maximum use is made of airspeed and position to keep the sequence flowing smoothly. Sure, free-style aerobatics is great stuff, but not for training, and not without a *thorough* background in basic aerobatics first.

It is not my purpose here to write a primer on aerobatic flying; you should invest in one or more good manuals already available for that. I am interested in making sure you are aware of the need for such manuals, as well as why aerobatic instruction is important. In most standard airplanes, airspeed control is rather critical and the unusual attitudes of aerobatic flying make this even more important. A clean airplane, such as a Bonanza, simply cannot be left nose-down for more than a few seconds; the airspeed quickly gets into the yellow arc and heads for the redline, where disaster awaits the unknowledgeable yanking on the controls. Should V_{ne} (redline airspeed) be exceeded substantially, a fatal control surface flutter might develop; loss of a control surface usually makes a recovery impossible.

Learning aerobatics involves knowing that such dangers exist and how to combat them. If airspeed is already plentiful, a nose-down attitude calls for the throttle to be cut to idle *immediately* to lessen speed buildup. If the nose is nearing a vertical attitude, on the other hand, and a tailslide is not desired, some thought has to be given to making a controlled exit from the straight-up position before all flying speed is lost. If a maneuver involves inverted flight, somebody is going to have to keep the nose up and roll the airplane back into normal flight without letting the airplane take matters into its own hands. Most importantly, spins need to be practiced so they can be recognized and stopped when they occur inadvertently, such as when attempting to half-roll off the top of a loop.

Learning aerobatics is a fine challenge, a great feeling of having a oneness with the aircraft and true mastery of anything the equipment can do. But it is also a skill to be acquired properly, with full awareness of the dangers involved.

Chapter 38

Taming the Tailwheel

As the decade of the '40s drew to a close, the assortment of airplanes at a typical airport looked quite a bit different from those seen today. The great majority of aircraft were taildraggers, so much so that tailwheel landing gear was then termed "conventional" gar. Flying a taildragger in those days was not considered the mark of a hairy-chested individualist, merely part of the accepted order of things, just as was strapping on a parachute as a student practiced spins before being allowed to solo. You learned to fly with a tailwheel, and when you bought a new airplane it would also probably have a tailwheel. Actually, the "hot" ships of the day were the ones with nosewheels—Bonanzas and Navions. They and a mildly popular prewar design, the Ercoupe, made up most of the tricycle gear population.

Out in Wichita, a small lightplane manufacturer by the name of Cessna was offering a complete line of three airplanes, all with tailwheels—the two-place 140, the four-place 170, and the ultimate luxury ship, the 195. There were speculations of a new design, perhaps to be called the 180, which was to be introduced as part of the Fiftieth Anniversary of Flight in 1953. Naturally, it would be a taildragger. Meanwhile, Bill Piper's bustling Lock Haven factory was turning out Cubs and Pacers, but some folks talked about a new Piper they had seen being tested, a Pacer with a nosewheel instead of a tailwheel.

The rest is history. Piper brought out the Tri-Pacer in 1951, and it sold like hotcakes as soon as pilots found out what they'd been missing. Cessna saw the light, and in 1955 the 172 was born, followed closely by the 182. In successive years, tailwheel airplanes have shrunk in numbers, and many wild tales have grown from the mystique surrounding the older designs. New fliers were told

"You're not really a pilot until you can handle one of these babies," and nosegear-trained pilots who sampled a taildragger found that they did have a lot to learn.

"Why the tailwheel?" asks the novice pilot. When hard pressed, most taildragger pilots find it difficult to answer. Sure, less weight and drag, better prop clearance on the ground, less trouble in the bush country, all these are cited as reasons, but few pilots flying taildraggers actually need these slight advantages, so it boils down to a simple preference. The same kind of person who likes to shift his own gears in his car, or control the exposure of his camera, will like a tailwheel airplane simply for the joy of having mastered it. Pilots are like that, and the pleasure of doing something for no real reason is one of the joys of living.

The Transition

How difficult is the transition to tailwheel for the pilot who has never flown anything but nosegear airplanes? If he was taught properly and has kept increasing his skill, the transition will be relatively simple. For the not-so-sharp pilot, it will be thrilling—both for him *and* his instructor.

As with most new subjects, a little preflight study of basic theory helps hasten the inflight learning. A tailwheel landing gear is arranged with the center of gravity of the airplane behind the main gear, so that enough weight rests on the tailwheel to hold it down and

Fig. 38-1. The Way We Were. This J3C Piper Cub, as well as the Taylorcraft and Cessna 180 behind it, are examples of how airplanes used to be built. The aft-CG configuration means touchy ground handling for the uninitiated, requiring a proper checkout.

Fig. 38-2. This classic Cessna 195, the last of the round-engine Cessnas, flies just like any airplane in the air; on the ground, however, the pilot had better be prepared for tailwheel characteristics.

provide steering friction. The tricycle-geared airplane, on the other hand, has the CG located in front of the main gear, and the nosewheel supports a portion of the weight when at rest. This placement of the CG is an important point, since it affects the stability of the airplane when it is in motion on the ground. With the nosegear arrangement, the CG acts to pull the airplane back to a straight path if the longitudinal axis becomes misaligned with the ground track. But the taildragger's CG, which is "pushing" the main gear, adds exactly the wrong force when displaced, tending to get the tail around in front of the main gear. If not controlled, this is the start of the famous "groundloop" so colorfully embellished in hangar-flying tales.

In a classic groundloop, the tail swings around in a tight circle, the inside wing rises and perhaps the inside main tire leaves the ground, and the tail comes up as the airflow no longer passes over the elevators and the panic-stricken pilot applies the brakes. The airplane can come to rest inverted in extreme cases, usually without injury to the occupants until they unfasten their seat belts.

To stop the groundloop before it goes too far, chop any throttle, use only the outside brake, apply full aileron to the inside of the turn, and pin the stick full back.

176

Respect!

Simply put, the tailwheel airplane has limitations, just as do all airplanes, and the pilot must respect them. You must not allow a slight swerve to go unchecked, as you might with a nosewheel. Instead, constant attention to maintaining a straight ground path is required. Small corrections, made early in the game, are needed to prevent a groundloop from ever beginning. The poor ability of the small castering tailwheel to resist a crosswind component and the generally slower touchdown speeds of the taildragger combine to mean somewhat less crosswind can be handled by the inexperienced pilot than with tricycle gear.

Finally, control of the ground handling situation requires that the tailwheel be in constant, firm contact with the surface; otherwise, the main wheels will be free to choose their own path to travel. Placement of the elevators to maintain this contact is important, and most of the time the stick should be held full back so the elevators will be up to catch propwash and headwind.

To begin with, the pilot of a taildragger must have his seat properly adjusted. He should be able to push full travel with the rudder pedals without stretching, yet not be so close as to stab a toe-brake accidentally. Land a nosewheel airplane with brakes applied and you merely stop quickly in a cloud of expensive smoke; land a taildragger with brakes on and you will stop even quicker—inverted! Some older designs have heel-actuated brakes, a real pain because the rudder bar moves but the brake pedal doesn't, and at full travel it's difficult to reach both rudder and brake. But the arrangement does have the advantage of keeping the pilot away from applying the brakes unintentionally.

Taxi, Then Fly

During the first attempt at taxiing, you may feel that you are not in full command of the airplane, and probably you aren't. That's why you have a CFI with you. While a large pneumatic tailwheel tire and properly adjusted steering gear will give almost as much directional control as a spring-steered nosewheel, the positive, crisp control just isn't there. Stay with the airplane, using early rudder application to keep the direction desired, and try to use less and less control travel as you gradually catch up with the airplane. As a last resort, use the brakes to stop a swerve that has gotten out of control, but don't steer with the brakes exclusively. Remember, keep that stick back to hold the tail down, especially when the brakes are being applied.

A certain amount of forward visibility on the ground is sacrificed with the tailwheel configuration, so you may need to peer around the cowling and S-turn during taxi to clear the path ahead. Enjoy it. That bit about the steely-eyed birdman leaning from the cockpit is part of the taildragger mystique. Taxi slowly—no faster than a running walk—and when taxiing downwind move the stick forward, deflecting the elevators downward so the wind will hold the tail down. Park headed into the wind for the runup, so the wind and propwash are both available to hold the tail down. Keep the stick back during the runup, and don't let the airplane creep, because abrupt braking lightens the tail.

Checklist completed, it's time to have a go at high-speed taxiing. Use the runway (or a wide taxiway) for some mock takeoffs and landings, running up to near liftoff speed then cutting the throttle and slowing to a stop. As the throttle is fully opened and speed picks up, the tail will rise and the rudder, rather than the tailwheel, will play an increasingly important role in controlling the airplane. The tail can be held down for positive steering at first, but you may find it more helpful to get the tail up quickly for a better view of the runway ahead, which will aid your perception of misalignment. Don't worry if the instructor has to bail you out of some wild swerves at first; that's the way everyone began in the early days. Remember, use small corrections to catch errors early. Less and less rudder travel will be required as speed picks up. Constantly "walking," or fanning the rudder, was once taught as a coordination device, but it should not be necessary as soon as you get the feel of the airplane.

The tailwheel airplane is not finished flying until it is brought to a complete stop, much more so than a nosegear airplane, so don't go to sleep in the final stages of the rollout. Some large rudder displacements may be necessary at the last, aided by a touch of brake. Don't try to turn before slowing to taxi speed, or you may induce a swerve that is beyond the tailwheel and brakes' ability to stop.

Having been emboldened by the high-speed taxi runs, you are now game for the full takeoff and landing, which is straightforward enough after the aforementioned preparation. Apply full throttle, hold a very straight track as the tail comes up, and keep the tail low by adding back pressure as speed picks up. The airplane will "float" off the runway at a much slower speed this way, and naturally you could let the tail come up higher for a faster liftoff speed in gusty crosswinds, if desired.

178

The Landing

Once in the air, you will find no difference in the aircraft's handling over a similar tricycle-geared ship. Eventually, however, the landing must be faced, and it comes in two types: three-point or "wheel" landing. The three-point or full-stall landing is normally used at first due to its slower touchdown speed and immediate transition to a taxi. The wheel, or tail-high, landing is used for better control in gusty winds since touchdown is made at a higher speed and is quite often preferred by taildragger aficionados.

The three-point landing is achieved by flaring just above the runway and holding the airplane off until the stick is completely back and all flying speed is lost. At this point all three wheels touch down and you are taxiing. If the touchdown is misaligned, expect some nervous moments straightening out the incipient groundloop. If the airplane is allowed to touch down tail-high—a common habit of sloppy nosewheel pilots who haven't done a soft-field landing since their flight test—the tail will drop due to its inertia, increasing the angle of attack and lifting the airplane right back into the air. If you then shove the nose down, contacting the runway at an even higher rate of sink, you'll get another rebound, worse than before. By this time somebody had better get the throttle in hand and initiate a go-around or the result will be one mangled airplane.

When the airplane bounces from a too-hasty touchdown, level off by using a little forward stick, or perhaps by just easing off back pressure, until gravity takes over and the airplane again starts sinking to the runway. If the bounce is quite severe, a little application of power might be wise to keep the airplane out of a stall and soften the sink rate. As the airplane settles back to earth, bring the stick full back to the stop before the tires touch and hold it there during the rollout. Remember, never be too proud to go around—especially in a taildragger.

The wheel landing is a touchdown on the mainwheels with flying speed still available, offering better control to battle winds. By keeping the wings at a low or negative angle of attack, no bounce results even though touchdown speed is above normal stall. The tail must be lowered eventually, but you can at least delay this moment of crosswind vulnerability rather than handling touchdown and steering chores all at the same time.

The secret of achieving a tail-high touchdown without bouncing sky-high (the natural tendency, as we've just discussed) is to never let the tail get down in the first place. This means a slightly faster approach speed may be needed, so the flare to stop the aircraft's sink

Fig. 38-3. Executing a tail-high "wheel landing," this Cessna 185 pilot retains good control during the touchdown. As airspeed slows, the tailwheel will sink into the grass, taking over steering duties.

will be achieved without going into a nose-high attitude. With the airplane in level flight just above the runway, only a slight relaxing of back pressure is required to roll the tires smoothly onto the speeding pavement.

There must be little or no sink remaining at the moment of contact, because a sudden vertical deceleration will tend to lower the unsupported tail and trigger a rebound. As speed slows during rollout, more pressure will be needed to hold the tail up, and the tail should be lowered for good steering before rudder control is lost. Naturally, use little or no brakes while the tail is up.

The wheel landing may require some practice, but no taildragger pilot should fly without knowing how to land tail-high. Spring-gear Cessnas or Pipers with new shock cords will bounce gloriously if a wheel landing is attempted with an ill-timed shove on the stick in an effort to get the tail back up. Go around or transition into a three-point landing, and try it again, next time endeavoring not to let the tail get much below level flight before touching down. Don't worry; the airflow will apply more and more pressure to keep the tail down as it rises, so you aren't liable to nose over by wheeling it on as long as you stay off the brakes and avoid soft runways.

So now you're a complete pilot, and you've learned to fly an airplane the way it was a half a century or so ago. Nosewheels are wonderful in stiff crosswinds, and they do make the pilot's job much easier, but the tailwheel airplane will make you a better pilot, and a more confident one. Enjoy it.

Chapter 39

High-Performance Checkout

When you're ready to take the inevitable step into larger, heavier, and faster airplanes, it is only logical to get checked out by a qualified CFI. Traditionally, the decision to seek formal training was left to the pilot involved, but some time ago the FAA decided that relying on common-sense checkouts for bigger aircraft types was creating a safety problem too great to be overlooked. While insurance companies almost universally require checkouts by a CFI, there were still the rare cases of a wealthy lightplane pilot purchasing a P-51 Mustang, crawling into the cockpit, and launching himself into oblivion—all quite legally, of course, because he was operating within the limitations specified on his license—"Airplane, Single-Engine, Land."

Thou Shalt Not . . .

FAR Part 61.31(e) was added in 1973 to require a logged one-time transition course before a pilot could fly aircraft of two categories: airplanes with more than 200 horsepower or airplanes with retractable landing gear, flaps, and controllable propeller. While the later three items are always installed in most cases, this brings up an interesting question: Would a retractable-geared airplane with a fixed-pitch prop and no flaps (a KR-1 homebuilt, for example) require a complex-airplane endorsement? No, according to FAA sources, because *all three* elements aren't installed.

As regulations go, this one is not particularly burdensome. Any CFI-Airplane can take care of the requirement, which is simply an endorsement in the pilot's logbook that he or she has been found competent to fly high-performance airplanes. According to current interpretations, a checkout in either type of airplane meets the FAR requirement. If a pilot demonstrated proficiency in a retractable with less than 200 horsepower, for example, he would be qualified to fly a Cessna 182 with 230 horsepower, and an endorsement gained in the 182 would suffice for flying a Piper Arrow of 180 hp, even though that aircraft has retractable gear and a straight-Skylane does not. Of course, any sensible pilot would get some qualified person to ride with him when transitioning to a new type of aircraft, particularly if it involves a performance step-up, so the regulation hardly takes the place of common-sense practice.

Older pilots enjoy grandfather rights. If they can show they have had experience in the over-200-hp or retractable-gear airplanes before November 1, 1973, they do not have to seek a logbook endorsement. Also, there is no further requirement for training if the pilot goes into another type of high-performance airplane, such as from a Cessna 182 to a Cherokee Six, or from an Arrow to a Mooney. Rightly so, the FARs assume that a pilot will have received the basic background knowledge for operating a high-performance airplane, and will therefore be able to transition intelligently to other types. It has always been basic premise of American aviation that judgment cannot be created by regulation, and that the FARs only provide a basic framework to be fleshed out with common sense. For this reason, insurance requirements usually fill the void to protect underwriters against pilots who lack enough judgment to seek a type checkout on their own.

The Checkout

What should you expect—or perhaps demand—when seeking this endorsement? Even more so than with primary training, book study must preceed actual flight, because you will be dealing with a more complicated machine. Sleep with the aircraft handbook until you know the airplane's systems, performance capabilities, and limitations, as well as the normal and emergency operating procedures. Time spent in ground study will save needless airwork, and with the increased expense of flying bigger birds, this only makes economic sense. To make sure you have gleaned the important points from the handbook, a good, stiff oral quiz should be part of the program.

Typical of such an oral was the one covering a Beech Sierra for which a local pilot sought a high-performance endorsement. I wanted to know the maximum landing gear *retraction* speed, as well as the V_{ge}; although it is not usually an operating hazard for the Sierra pilot, knowing that such a speed exists shows the pilot has done his homework. I also asked how much fuel would be in the tanks when the gauges read "full," another test of his preparation—the Sierra's tanks hold 26 usable gallons apiece, but only 20 gallons are needed to give a full reading on the gauges. To make sure the pilot was familiar with fuel-injected engines, I inquired about the starting procedure for a hot engine. I also wanted to know how the landing gear system operated, and the emergency gear extension procedure. How much cabin payload is permitted with fuel tanks full, and how is it to be distributed? What are the runway requirements under adverse conditions of temperature and elevation? These questions were typical of the oral checkout for a light retractable.

An oral covering an endorsement gained in a heavy-horsepower single, such as a Cherokee Six or a Cessna 206, similarly delves into the systems and operating details. How does loading affect performance? How heavy can the sole two occupants of the airplane be without exceeding forward CG limits? How light can the front seat occupants be before the aft CG limit is reached with a full load of average people? Where is the battery located? How does one manage the fuel tanks of the Cherokee Six? *Know thy airplane* is the criterion, and more airplane means more to know.

Because a more complex avionics package is normally part of the higher-performance airplane, some time is spent on radios; puzzling over the audio panel in a faster airplane can get a tyro pilot into trouble before he realizes it.

To become familiar with the one new power control, the constant speed prop must be seen as a "gearshift" control; low gear, or low pitch, provides high rpm for takeoff, a second "gear" selects a cruising-climb setting, and a high "gear" or higher pitch setting is used for low-rpm cruising power. The power lever—which is still the throttle—is moved to a lower power setting before each reduction of rpm so the slower-turning engine will not be "lugging" with nearly full throttle. Manifold pressure is the only reference available for adjusting the throttle. The propeller control is returned to low pitch (high rpm) position just prior to landing so that the engine will be ready to respond to full throttle in the event of a go-around.

During the actual inflight training I watch to see if the transitioning pilot is learning to keep up with the faster plane. Bigger airplanes with heavier wing loadings tend to be more stable than light trainers. This makes them somewhat easier to fly, but their very stability can cause them to sink right on into the ground if the pilot gets behind the airplane on a landing approach.

Flight maneuvers used to transition the pilot to high-performance flying include such old standbys as steep 720° turns and slow flight. The steep turns increase the critical nature of control inputs to speed up the process of getting the feel of the airplane, while slow flight teaches the pilot what to expect in the traffic pattern, particularly when combined with flap and /or landing gear extension while holding airspeed and altitude.

Stalls are a natural outgrowth of slow-flight practice, and must be demonstrated from all normal flight conditions. Usually the meanest configuration will be a partial-power, full-dirty landing approach stall, a situation where a high-performance airplane usually gives little warning of imminent disaster until the bottom falls out. Instrument flight is also worked into the transition, commensurate with the pilot's ratings; a private pilot-VFR will need to demonstrate only basic survival skills, while an instrument-rated individual will get some approach work.

Around the Pattern

Takeoff and landing practice is the payoff, and nowhere is a tendency to get behind the bigger, faster airplane more evident than in the traffic pattern. Increased torque makes right rudder application more pronounced during takeoff; failing to anticipate this causes frequent deviations from the centerline. A climb-power reduction takes a extra second or two because there are now two controls to be adjusted, and a fast climb rate brings the airplane up to altitude quickly—often before the new-to-type pilot is ready for it. Upon reaching pattern altitude, power should be reduced for the downwind leg so the airspeed will be kept compatible with normal training-aircraft speeds to avoid conflicts in the pattern and make it easier to transition to the landing approach.

The downwind leg, or the initial pattern entry just prior to descent if a base leg or straight-in approach is made, is the place to have a habitual prelanding routine established. GUMP is still a good short checklist: G-gas on proper tank and boost pump on if needed; U—undercarriage knob moved to the down position; M—mixture control returned to full rich if not already done so; and P—propeller pitch set to high rpm (some pilots prefer to leave the prop alone until short final to avoid an increase in noise level).

After running the GUMP check, a power reduction is made to an appropriate approach setting, usually 10 to 12 inches of manifold pressure, to allow a normal-size pattern to be flown. Power approaches are *de regle* because power-off glides would be short and steep in those highly wing-loaded airplanes. At the time of the first power reduction a check of the gear-down lights should be made to see if the gear has completed its cycle. Speed is reduced to a figure equivalent to 1.3 times the stall speed in landing configuration, plus 10 knots for maneuvering. Partial flaps are extended no later than the base leg, or about two miles out on a straight-in approach.

On final approach, speed is reduced by adding full flap, and a stabilized approach is sought; speed should be constant at $1.3\ V_{so}$ with power adequate to carry the airplane to the runway without further adjustment. One should strive to avoid letting high (over 500 fpm) sink rates develop on short final, a sneaky condition that can cause a high-performance airplane to sink through the bottom of a last-minute flare to make a hard touchdown.

A few hours spent in initial transition training for high-performance airplanes is well worth the time, because the pilot who has not learned to stay ahead of his airplane is an accident going somewhere to happen. Take advantage of such a program to sharpen basic flying skills, and use the same checkout procedure whenever moving into another complex airplane, even though further checkouts might not be required by the FARs.

Chapter 40

Doing It for Money

As most private and even student pilots know, the next level of pilot certificate beyond the basic private license is entitled "Commercial Pilot." The commercial certificate is required if pilots are to receive money for their services, but the rating also is a laudable goal for anyone interested in bettering his pilot skills, whether or not he might actually be contemplating a career in aviation.

Requirements for the commercial certificate are outlined in FAR Part 61, with additional information contained in AC 61-55, a small pamphlet available from the Government Printing Office or at most flight schools. As you will discover, you need a second-class medical certificate, a passing grade on the commercial written exam, and 250 hours of various types of pilot experience. The first two requirements should be tackled first; obviously, there is no need to spend good money for training if you can't get by the second class medical exam, and having the written passed places you under a certain time constraint, which encourages aggressive flight training.

It was not always necessary to have 250 hours for the commercial ticket; as a matter of fact, I took my first charter trip at the tender age of 222 hours. The minimum time was increased from 200 to 250 hours in 1973, when FAR Part 61 was extensively revised. This was done to assure that commercial pilots would add enough hours to get an instrument rating, which became mandatory for unrestricted commercial flying at that time. It is not true, however, that an instrument rating is an *absolute* prerequisite for a commercial ticket. Recognizing that some paying jobs can be done safely without instrument training—such as aerial application, sightseeing rides and local photography flights—the FAA retained a limited VFR commercial endorsement that allows carriage of passengers for hire within a 50-mile radius and during daylight hours only.

Help Us Help You

So that we can better provide you with the practical information you need, please take a moment to complete and return this card.

1. **I am interested in books on the following subjects:**

☐ architecture & design   ☐ electronics
☐ automotive   ☐ engineering
☐ aviation   ☐ hobbies & crafts
☐ business & finance   ☐ how-to, do-it-yourself
☐ computer, mini & mainframe   ☐ military history
☐ computer, micros   ☐ nautical
☐ other_____

2. **I own/use a computer:**

☐ Apple/Macintosh_____
☐ Commodore_____
☐ IBM_____
☐ Other_____

3. **This card came from TAB book (no. or title):**

_____

4. **I purchase books from/by:**

☐ general bookstores
☐ technical bookstores   ☐ telephone
☐ college bookstores   ☐ electronic mail
☐ mail   ☐ hobby stores
          ☐ art materials stores

Comments _____

_____

_____

Name _____

Address _____

City _____

State/Zip _____

TAB BOOKS Inc.

Another exemption from the instrument proviso was granted to airtaxi operators who fly in remote areas far from navigational aids and even paved airports. For these bush pilots an instrument rating is rather a useless attainment, so the FAA decided to let back-country air-taxi operators go ahead and hire good bush pilots who lack an IFR ticket.

For unlimited commercial privileges, however, an instrument rating is still necessary, and most professional flying jobs are closed to noninstrument pilots. It is wise to work the instrument curriculum into the program first; if you have accumulated the 200 hours needed for the instrument ticket, but not the 250 hours needed for the commercial, the time would be well spent getting the instrument rating. On the other hand, if you are seeking a commercial ticket for personal purposes only, you may wish to save more than half the cost by going after a limited commercial.

What's Commercial?

When do you actually need a commercial certificate? Basically, if you get paid for flying the airplane, you are operating commercially and need the license. If you are a salesman and the company doesn't *specifically* tell you to cover your territory in an airplane, you may legally make your rounds on a private ticket. Likewise, you can demonstrate an airplane to a prospective purchaser on a private license, because then you are a salesperson and not a hired pilot. However, if you are required to haul cargo or personnel for your company, even though no charges or bonus renumeration is involved, you are being paid to fly and should have a commercial ticket.

Don't assume the acquisition of a commercial certificate gives you the right to haul people around the country for hire. You will also need an FAR Part 135 Air Taxi Certificate, which means your entire operation—including airplanes, flight manuals, offices and record-keeping—must be inspected periodically in addition to being staffed by qualified pilots. Remember, the operator must hold an air taxi certificate while you as the pilot must hold a Commercial Certificate; both requirements must be met to fly a charter.

If you are an airplane owner, you may receive a break on your insurance premium with a commercial ticket, although it probably won't be enough to pay for the training. Mostly, you'll take pride in the fact that you've chosen to upgrade yourself to a higher standard of demonstrated proficiency. In truth, a very sharp private pilot with 50 hours could probably perform the commercial maneuvers well enough to pass the checkride, but there's more to flying commercially than just getting twice as good as you were for the private ticket.

Requirements

Assuming you're healthy, at least 18 years of age, and have passed the written, what else is needed? Disregarding the instrument rating, the underlying commercial requirements are for at least 100 hours of pilot-in-command time, 50 hours of which must be cross-country time, which means you landed at least 50 nautical miles from the departure point including one trip with landings at three points, each 200 nautical miles from the others. Fifty hours of dual instruction are needed, with at least 10 hours logged in preparation for the commercial flight test (all previous dual counts toward the 50). At least five hours of night time are needed, including 10 landings, and 10 hours of instrument instruction are required. These apparently redundant night and instrument requirements are a holdover from the days when no formal night training was needed for a private ticket, and an instrument rating was something to be sought only after one began flying commercially. You must have logged 10 hours in an airplane with retractable gear, flaps, and a controllable propeller.

Aside from the instrument rating curriculum, which you may complete earlier or skip entirely, it would be normal to expect to run up 25 to 30 hours in preparation for the commercial flight test. The concurrent ground training will concentrate on detailed knowledge of aircraft performance, systems, and loading requirements. During the oral portion of the exam, expect to be grilled thoroughly on every aspect of safe piloting; if you're going to charge for your services, you are expected to be worth your pay.

What's New?

In addition to the maneuvers you performed for the private license, there are a few added maneuvers on the commercial test, specifically the steep power turn, spiral about a point, lazy 8, chandelle, and accuracy landing. The steep turn is to be performed with precision while holding at least a 50° bank with power increased to maintain airspeed, and the spiral involves correcting for wind drift while descending about a point on the ground, using steepest banks of 50° and 55° and circling a selected point rather than an area. Lazy 8s are a test of your ability to fly a predetermined pattern of loops above and below the horizon in reference to a fixed point, using smooth and delicate control inputs. The chandelle is a steep 180°

climbing turn, using the stored energy of the airplane's speed to gain the maximum altitude possible as airspeed bleeds off during the turn; this is an exercise in planning, demonstrating your ability to think ahead of your airplane to make it arrive in a certain flight condition at the end of the maneuver.

Accuracy landings also demonstrate planning, as you attempt to place the aircraft in a normal touchdown beyond and within 200 feet of a given line, with no last-minute corrections from the throttle. Speed control, drag adjustments, power reduction, and turn placement all must be balanced carefully to bring the aircraft down on target.

The old standbys—crosswind takeoffs and landings, soft and short field operation, slow flight, stalls, and forced landings—are all in the commercial curriculum, with slight changes added to test increased skill and with performance tolerances more or less halved as compared with the private checkride. For example, if altitude can wander 100 feet on the private ride, you'll get only 50 feet of tolerance on the commercial test. Expect distractions from the examiner, who attempts to place you under the stresses paying passengers might generate. Stalls from all flight conditions are performed, but recovery is to begin in the "imminent" phase of the stall. It will also be necessary to demonstrate your proficiency in a complex airplane (retractable gear, flaps, and controllable propeller) on the flight test, normally just a few minutes of basic maneuvers.

For the dedicated and serious student of aviation, the commercial license is not too difficult to attain. However, it takes a certain amount of desire to improve yourself, and while you may not have visions of flying for a living, it's nice to be able to hold in your hands a tangible reward for your efforts. Well-paying jobs in aviation are scarce and highly sought after, but the ability to fly for your company might make extra points on a resume, even in non-aviation employment. Consider adding the next level of competence to your license, especially if you're already instrument rated. It's a great exercise for jaded flying skills.

Chapter 41

The Instrument
Rating: Is It Worth It?

Eventually, most private pilots who are reasonably unimpeded by financial constraints will consider getting an instrument rating added to their licenses. After being weathered out of a few choice trips, seeing other pilots depart through a cloud layer, or hearing a fellow airman brag about the joys of IFR flight, it's only natural to want to join the club.

Before you plunge off into pursuit of the instrument ticket, however, it would be a good idea to analyze the cost /benefit ratio in your own operation. Many new instrument pilots are disappointed with the increase in utility they have gained, and they wind up flying very few IFR hours despite having the legal ability to do so. For some pilots an instrument ticket will be an under-utilized luxury, while for others it is a virtual necessity. Let's see which category comes closest to matching your situation.

Certainly an instrument rating would be a worthwhile goal if you have time and money to spare for self-improvement. You will gain valuable insight into controlled-airspace operation, which will make you a safer and more poised pilot. Your weather wisdom will be increased and you will possess a valuable "escape" tool in case you get suckered into a bad weather situation. If you plan to go on to seek a Commercial Certificate someday, you may as well plan to get the IFR ticket as soon as you meet the 200-hour total experience requirement, since an instrument rating is nearly a prerequisite.

What It Takes to Get the Rating

These advantages notwithstanding, the fact remains that a lot of instrument pilots don't use their rating enough to justify its cost. You should figure on spending at least as much money for instrument training as you did to get the private ticket, if not a bit more; a more expensive airplane and avionics package is required for instrument work. A total of 40 hours of instrument time is needed to qualify for the rating, at least half of which must be dual, although it has been my experience that somewhat more than 20 hours of dual are required to make a capable instrument pilot. Half of these hours can be logged at the controls of an approved ground simulator, saving valuable airplane time while you develop a scan pattern and learn how to fly an approach for the first time. However, there's no substitute for the *real* airplane, in *real* weather.

Instruction must be given and proficiency demonstrated in all three types of commonly used instrument approaches, i.e., those using the ILS, VOR, and ADF. Therefore, the airplane must have enough equipment to fly these procedures (or a suitable simulation must be provided). At least one cross-country flight covering more than 200 nautical miles must be included in the training, utilizing all three types of approach, each at a different airport. You should plan on flying between two and three hours at a session when you're immersed in instrument training to permit more approaches to be practiced and to allow for shuttling between airports.

First, however, there is a written test to be passed, something that might as well be tackled before flight training begins in earnest. There's nothing tricky about the test, but you do have to know the material. You can prepare equally well with a home-study course, an integrated FBO program, or with the help of a weekend cram course, whichever suits your study habits. You may as well buy at least a one-time set of NOS charts and approach plates, since that's what the FAA's written tests use for examples. Consider Jeppesen coverage only after you pass the written.

What the Rating Will and Won't Do

Now, consider what you will be getting for your investment. Too many VFR pilots think their life will become simpler with an instrument rating, because they can fly with fewer restrictions. *Wrong*. Life gets *more* complicated, not less so, because more and weightier decisions must be made. In return for the privilege of flying through clouds, you sacrifice your freedom to depart, terminate, and alter your flight as you choose. Each action is carefully controlled to preclude conflicts with unseen traffic. You *ask* for a clearance to depart, for a change in altitude, for a new routing; less spontaneity is possible.

Likewise, it is all too often presumed that weather can no longer delay a flight. *Wrong again*. The instrument aviator can fly in lower weather minimums, but there is still plenty of weather bad enough to cause a cancellation; zero-zero fog halts even airline traffic. Even if the weather is up to the 200-feet and one-half mile of ILS minimums, when you're a new or rusty instrument pilot you may want to wait for 500 feet of ceiling while you're gaining your precision. Thunderstorms, icing, low-level turbulence, widespread near-minimums weather with no alternate airports in reach, or an airplane with limited avionics—these are just a few of the things that can keep an instrument-rated pilot on the ground despite the rating in his pocket.

Remember, little airplanes are really meant to fly only in warm stratus clouds. Turbine-powered equipment, on the other hand, can expand a pilot's range of altitudes and offer a fast climb rate through the lower crud, advantages we little-airplane people don't have. The airlines fly in almost any weather conditions, but remember that they use *two* pilots, with the best available equipment, over familiar routes, with extensive ground support—and they *still* overfly or cancel some stops at times. You, in a single-pilot, limited-performance, random-routing operation, must also expect to let good judgment cause some cancellations, even with an IFR ticket.

Will It Pay?

If you fly quite a few cross-country hours in the course of a year, or live in a part of the country subject to frequent stretches of fairly localized below-VFR weather, you'll certainly benefit from the instrument rating. You can fly perhaps 75 percent of your trips without it, and maybe 90 percent with it; the other 10 percent will require known-icing certification and turbocharging to achieve.

Add up the cost of getting the rating; include the time lost from work, the actual training expense, and perhaps the cost of ferry flights to and from a suitable instructor. To this add the tab for any additional equipment and inspections required to bring your airplane up to IFR standards, if the airplane isn't already in shape. Don't forget the expense of instrument charts and the periodic refresher training needed to stay current. From the total thus far you can deduct any insurance premium savings resulting from adding an instrument rating.

Now estimate the number of extra trips you *honestly* could have made last year, given the capability provided by your airplane's performance. The importance of these additional flights determines if it is practical for you to go after an instrument ticket. If you're short of loose cash to spend in getting your airplane up to speed, or if you don't plan to fly all that many hours cross-country, maybe you'll opt to stay VFR for now. You need not apologize for your decision, and you can take comfort in your simpler life style.

On the other hand, the possession of an instrument ticket does give you an extra option to play. You can press on with deteriorating weather conditions just a bit longer than a VFR pilot, knowing that you can pick up the microphone and get a clearance. You can leave a socked-in airport a few hours earlier when conditions first start to improve, rather than waiting for the sun to break out. Perhaps best of all, it is a considerable comfort to know that you can always leave this forlorn weathered-in field if you want to work at it hard enough; the VFR pilot has no such ability, and whether or not you always choose to exercise the capability, it's nice to have it.

The additional knowledge and experience of instrument training is worth a lot. If you've never seen the world change from dingy gray to bright and sunny with a few thousand feet of altitude, or had the pleasure of being in perfect alignment with the approach lights as you slide out of the overcast, or enjoyed the luxury of spending a damp, rainy night at home with the family rather than somewhere in a motel, you can't really appreciate all the benefits of flying by instruments. Just remember the price tag, and decide if it's for you.

Chapter 42

What to Do with
Your New IFR Ticket

Congratulations, you've finally struggled through the written exam, a long, tiring flight training program, and a white-knuckles checkride. Now you possess an instrument rating and you would like to put it to work, but you don't quite know how to begin. You have been given the right to shoot a 200-and-one-half approach, but not the confidence to tackle it alone.

Well, join the club. Every new instrument pilot has had to go through the same things. Flight schools are very good at pumping out quick instrument ratings, but they often graduate students with no actual experience in flying through weather. Those who need an instrument ticket are usually busy, involved people, and they must take a concentrated course of instruction in order to complete the training at all. Unfortunately, this can lead to minimal competence and even less confidence, because the statistical probabilities are against encountering actual instrument weather in a short training program. There are no substitutes for hard rain on the windshield, a dark, wet cloud, and the trapped feeling of nearing minimums while still shrouded in stratus. It's different than when wearing a hood in the sunshine with a professional in the right seat, no doubt about it.

And yet you got the instrument rating to use, not to sit on, so you must get to work immediately gaining solo proficiency. Using instrument flying skills aids retention of the hard-won ability and builds confidence. Putting off that first solo venture into a cloud only makes it harder to face the inevitable, so don't wait even a week to start filing IFR, if possible. Naturally, there's a proper way to begin—by easing into it slowly.

First We Walk, Then We Run

When tackling your first local instrument approaches to build proficiency, establish minimums somewhat higher than those allowed by the approach plates; for non-precision approaches you might wait for conditions of 1000-foot ceiling and two miles visibility, and even for a full-ILS arrival you should have 500 feet and one mile for openers. This is not because you can't fly well enough to keep the needles centered if all goes well, but to cover yourself if you get slightly behind the airplane while handling the communications chores. In such a case, you could be forced to miss the approach unless you have marginal VFR underneath. Don't stick to clear days, however; you won't build confidence by filing IFR in the clear.

So with your pencil poised and your charts neatly folded, call for that first clearance solo; you'll probably find it easier than you thought. Unless you're operating in a terminal area, there will be few other airplanes on the frequency, and you'll receive immediate response to your call, unlike the hectic weekend traffic on VFR channels. Don't forget to turn the transponder on before takeoff, have the radials and frequencies pretuned before entering the clouds, and enjoy yourself. Breaking out into the clear and looking back at what you've come through is what it's all about, and it's a great feeling.

Departing Cross-Country

After polishing your cloud-flying skills close to home, prepare for IFR cross-country work. Hopefully you will have been making all VFR cross-countries on an IFR clearance to gain familiarity with ATC procedures as pilot-in-command. When you're ready for the real thing, don't bite off more than you can safely chew the first time out. A three-hour cross-country in the clouds with no autopilot is tiring even for an experienced pilot, especially when mixed with turbulence and a gnawing doubt about the wisdom of being there.

For your first instrument exposure beyond the local area, wait for a day when your departure airport is just beginning to open up and good weather is waiting a half-hour away. Without an instrument rating you would be forced to wait until conditions improved, but with the rating you may as well depart as soon as you have enough ceiling to organize your act before entering the clouds. As you are no doubt aware, non-commercial flights can legally depart under zero-zero conditions, but doing so is a calculated risk for competent pilots only, due to the inability to return if something goes wrong. Best to wait for a 500-foot ceiling and establish a definite improving trend to back up the reports of clearing conditions enroute. Knowing it'll get better as you go along always makes the trip seem shorter.

Do not be satisfied with a few minutes of actual IFR while

climbing to VFR conditions on top of the clouds. If you can see that a lower altitude will put you back into the stratus, ask for it; you need the practice, and you can always go back up into the clear if you feel the need to take a break. Don't plan on the tops being right where they were, however; the effects of terrain and air mass mixing can lift the cloud tops as the flight progresses. The tops are always a thousand feet higher than expected, and the icing level a thousand feet lower.

As your proficiency and confidence increase, you should begin filing into actual instrument conditions from a VFR departure, shooting approaches from an enroute environment, rather than the local approaches you have been executing to maintain currency. Always plan on having sufficient fuel to return to good weather, even when an alternate isn't required, just in case the destination weather goes down or an equipment failure prevents you from making the approach. In fact, you should have *two* alternates in mind, the one designated in your flight plan and another one to back it up. Never place yourself in a position with no out. Keep track of conditions at your alternates as well as the destination and you'll always have landing minimums somewhere within reach.

Finally, after first filing from bad weather into good, and then from good conditions into bad, you can start making intentional flights involving IMC from beginning to end. Keep your minimums-for-dispatch weather reasonable; don't blast off just as soon as the conditions along your route rise to landing minimums. Wait for a trend to be established that will give you reasonable safety and assurance that you can conduct the flight as planned. If you try to depart as soon as you get reports of bare-minimums weather, you run a good chance of having one or more of your key airports slip back down, leaving you with disrupted plans or perhaps no alternate within reach.

Watch the Weather

Learn to maintain an enroute weather watch. An instrument pilot has an excellent opportunity to watch weather develop, especially if he is on top or between layers; he can correlate this with the reports received. By continually checking weather at the destination and alternates, and applying your firsthand impressions, you can avoid being placed in a low-fuel situation or continuing into unsafe weather. A VFR pilot may be able to proceed on eyeball weather only, but an instrument pilot must supplement what he sees with fresh sequences, revised forecasts, and pilot reports if he wants to avoid nasty surprises.

There will always be weather that must not be tackled, even if you are current and confident. Thunderstorms are bad news and are usually best handled by staying VFR under the cloud base, where you can see and avoid the rain shafts. Don't make a habit of relying on ATC radar to guide you around embedded cells; someday the service might not be available. Likewise, the hazard of ice is better avoided than battled. Stay below the freezing level in clouds, climb into the clear air on top if able, or return to warm air behind you. The most important rule to remember when encountering icing conditions is *do something; don't just sit there.* Change your route or altitude to fly where the ice isn't, or don't fly at all. The final bane of instrument flying, dense ground fog, can be easily avoided by always having enough fuel to reach good weather—and knowing where the good weather is. Land short and top off the tanks if it appears fog might be a factor at your destination. Knowing you can cope with these weather hazards by making the right decisions increases your confidence in your ability.

To grow and improve as a green instrument pilot takes practice, not just simulator time and hood work. You must get your wings wet in the actual ATC environment and continue to do so as long as you seriously want to keep your instrument proficiency. So if you're new to instrument flying, or if it has been a long time since you flew in IMC, take an experienced hand along the first time to help handle the right seat chores, but get that hands-on practice you need.

Chapter 43

File IFR or Stay VFR?

I was being chided by an experienced fellow airman because I had arrived at a meeting by flying VFR under a low overcast. "LeRoy, you ought to know better than to go scud-running like that!" he admonished. I knew that whenever he encountered weather on a cross-country trip, he preferred to bore on through rather than avoid it. To him, the decision was always clear: File IFR or don't fly at all.

I accepted his advice in the spirit it had been given, but thought to myself how quickly we often judge someone's actions without considering the circumstances. What appears to be a dangerous, thoughtless action might be a reasonably safe and correct choice for a particular pilot, in a particular plane, on a particular day. The limitations of both the pilot and the machine must always be considered when deciding the best course of action.

How to Handle Weather

Thus it is with the question of how to handle weather. In training we tend to define weather as either good-VFR or hard-IFR, forgetting that in the real world we seldom enjoy such clear-cut definitions of weather. Most of the time inclement weather can be flown as either marginal-VFR or easy-IFR—such conditions as 1500-foot ceilings with five miles visibility, or 1000-foot and ten miles, or an unlimited ceiling with three miles visibility in haze. In these border-line cases, the pilot must make a decision about how best to handle the weather: Should he attempt VFR flight, or file IFR if he is instrument-rated?

We cannot overemphasize the need to *make* a decision. Murky weather is no time for vacillation; you need to make up your mind what you are going to do before you takeoff, and update your plan as the flight progresses. Sitting there scratching your head as you dodge the barely-VFR soup is silly, as is cancelling your IFR prematurely and later wishing you hadn't. To make intelligent decisions, you need hard information about the weather situation, so get a good briefing before takeoff. You need to know where the weather is worsening and where it is improving, what sort of system is affecting your route, and what is expected to occur with the passage of time. With this briefing, you can apply your observations and the hourly sequence reports to make assessments of your ability to complete the flight.

Go in the proper frame of mind to tackle weather. Forget about getting somewhere on schedule, or even getting somewhere in particular at all. Decide only if it is practical for you to set out along the route and be ready to divert without hesitation if the weather seems to be running behind the forecast. You can always reshuffle your business appointments or vacations—as long as you're around to do it.

Are You IFR or VFR?

If you are not instrument-rated or your airplane isn't suitably equipped, your life is less complicated. You simply should not begin any trip unless there is a reasonable assurance that you can get there free of clouds. Beyond this basic need you must add enough extra margin of cloud clearance and visibility to accommodate your navigation ability, your familiarity with the route, and the time of day.

If you are instrument-rated and equipped, you have the option of penetrating the weather if you so choose. While IFR may seem to be the way to go whenever conditions slip from CAVU, there could be reasons to avoid the ATC system. Not every airplane is able to handle every type of weather; a high-performance airplane with turbocharger and an oxygen bottle allows one to tackle conditions that would be hazardous in a light single. Perhaps the airplane you're flying has just begun to exhibit radio problems; it would be poor judgment to file into weather without being sure of your basic avionics. Perhaps there are reports of icing at the levels you would be forced to fly, and you are not equipped or inclined to tackle ice. Or radar may be reporting thunderstorms mixed into the soup. If you've recently had a brush with a cumulonimbus you may be unwilling to file IFR, preferring to avoid the storms visually.

Looking over the weather situation carefully allows the IFR pilot to make a decision about the mode of departure. If marginal VFR conditions exist locally, you may wish to depart IFR and seek a comfortable flight level on top or between layers, with the option to descend to VFR conditions if you encounter hazardous weather aloft. If you suspect dangerous weather at the altitudes required for IFR flight, you may want to leave VFR and go underneath, with the option to pick up a clearance if you encounter lower conditions enroute.

If you plan on climbing up through a broken layer to VFR-on-top, you may as well pick up a clearance to your destination; things have a way of getting busy if you just cruise into a terminal area VFR-on-top, and entering the system from a distance will smooth the handling of your arrival. And, if the weather situation worsens ahead, you're already in contact with ATC to expedite your options.

Sneaking Out? Be Careful

If you plan to leave VFR below the overcast, take care to choose a route that will permit you to plug into the ATC system later if needed. Sneaking up the valley VFR might not be so smart if you need to talk to Center in a hurry and you find you can't get high enough to make yourself heard. Or a direct course may take you so far from a communications outlet that voice and radar contact is impossible. If you remotely suspect you will need to file IFR, stay close to a route with ATC coverage, or airports with telephones.

Next, don't wait too long to file. We're getting all too many reports of instrument-rated pilots involved in marginal-VFR weather accidents, evidently because they thought they could make it on through without filing. Just as you did in your VFR days, tell yourself how low you're letting yourself go before you chicken out, and *do it*. The minimums are up to you; if you don't know exactly where you are, you'll probably give up sooner than you would if you were certain of your location or were just a few miles from home base. Just eyeball the elevation of the terrain and obstructions, assess your VFR skills, and say, "When I'm getting pushed down to *this* altitude, I'm getting out of here."

No two pilots will probably handle the situation in exactly the same manner. One of the saddest predicaments is an airplane with two captains, both of whom are equally experienced with nobody really in command. Often, the pilot in the left seat will head off into weather he really doesn't want to fly because he doesn't want to lose face in front of the other pilot. If I'm riding the right seat, I make sure the pilot knows he's in command and I'll ride with him, abiding by his decisions. He can ask my advice, but I'm not going to fly the airplane for him, and I don't want him to worry about what I'm thinking.

When Not to File

The heated discussion at the beginning of this chapter involved a stalled-out cold front over relatively flat terrain. I was flying a well-worn Skyhawk with vintage radios, equipped for localizer-only approaches, and the surface temperatures were only three or four degrees above freezing. Tops were expected to be around 9000 feet AGL. I was certainly not prepared for the ice I would get trying to climb above the weather, and the 'Hawk would run out of wind just as I was getting into the top of cumulus where the ice is often heaviest. Compounding the problem, there was no open weather nearby, only a promise of improvement at the destination.

The route under the clouds, by comparison, was well populated with VFR airports, where I could seek refuge, and an FSS was available for consultation in the middle of the route. So I elected to make this trip *under* the weather rather than through it. I did have a minimum altitude chosen, about 700 feet above the terrain in this case as visibility was relatively good below the cloud bases. At one point I was pushed almost down to my minimum and I was preparing to execute Plan B— a 180° turn to land and file IFR—but the clouds rose as reported shortly and it was not necessary.

For me, it had been a safe and easy trip. I was comfortable with the route and weather, but not everybody would have been, including my IFR-only friend. His pilotage navigation skills would have been rusty, and he would have been much more comfortable in the clouds with his radios and autopilot. Both of us were right, each in our own way. The best advice I can offer is to never continue with a flight if you don't feel comfortable doing so. Respect your own limitations—don't use someone else's.

Chapter 44

Regaining IFR Currency

If you're an instrument-rated pilot, you're no doubt aware of the requirement for recent IFR experience, as defined in FAR 61.57. Unlike some other recent-experience requirements, this FAR does not apply just to passenger-carrying privileges; you cannot fly in the clouds, solo or otherwise, unless you meet the currency standards of 61.57. You must have logged six hours of instrument time, actual or under the hood, within the past six months, including six instrument approaches.

An approved flight simulator may be used for up to three of the six hours, but the rest must be in an aircraft. If the inflight time was logged using a hood or other view-limiting device, you must show the name of the safety pilot in your logbook, although he or she need not personally sign the book. This safety pilot must be seated at the controls and hold at least a private pilot certificate.

There is no requirement that any dual be sought to regain instrument currency, as long as no more than a year has elapsed since you were last current. You can take your hood and safety pilot, fly off six instrument approaches and six hours of hood time, and be once again legal for IFR. You may not be safe, but at least you are covered under the FARs. Following two six-month periods, during one of which you were still current and during the next eligible for self-renewal of currency, you are barred from operating under IFR until taking an instrument competence ride with an instrument instructor.

Coming Back

So you look in the old logbook one day and see that you have had good luck during the past six months, avoiding IFR weather to the extent that you have not accumulated the required six hours with six approaches. Since you were current until recently, you have the option of getting the practice in on your own, without an instructor. Many instrument pilots prefer to take a period of dual and get an instrument competency endorsement instead of doing it themselves, particularly if it can be combined with a flight review. However, there is nothing wrong with self-improvement, properly done.

You need to accumulate 1) an instrument-equipped airplane; 2) a VFR day; 3) a safety pilot; and 4) a hood. The airplane need not actually be IFR certified, as long as the equipment is in good working order, since you will not be legal to enter instrument meteorological conditions anyway, unless your safety pilot is qualified and willing to assume command. Bear in mind that transponders must be certified every two years whether used for IFR or VFR, while the altimeter / static system check and VOR receiver test is for IFR purposes only.

Choose your safety pilot wisely. Would you trust your life to this person? That's exactly what you may be doing in relying on him to keep you separated from other traffic and deteriorating weather. If possible, a knowledgeable instrument pilot would be a wise choice for a safety pilot, someone with whom you can share recurrency training duties. He may be better at keeping abreast of the situation and anticipating your moves, while a VFR pilot would know very little about your intentions. If you feel this person could use a back-up, put another pair of eyes in the rear seat to help spot traffic.

Who Does What

Cockpit duties should be carefully defined before flying; a *too-*helpful safety pilot is no help at all, but he should be aware of what is expected of him. You should assume all communications chores relative to the IFR flight unless you are losing control of the airplane and the controller needs an immediate answer for safety reasons. Only then should your safety pilot help out. However, VFR traffic advisories are the safety pilot's responsibility, and he should be ready to handle the "Got 'im" reports. He should not bother you with "We've got one off to the right about a mile," unless avoidance maneuvering is likely; if it's just a topic of conversation, you've got enough to do under the hood without the small talk. Naturally, if he says "I've got it" you will release the controls to him, but wait for an acknowledging shake of the control column so you know he's talking about the airplane, not the traffic he's just spotted.

As long as your safety pilot is a current IFR aviator, file an IFR flight plan; you need practice in operating within the system, not just keeping the airplane right side up. In addition, more expeditious handling will be given your requests if you are operating on a clearance, rather than popping up VFR to shoot an approach.

Plan on getting in as many varied types of approaches as possible: ILS front course, ILS back course, VOR circling, VOR straight-in, ADF, RNAV, VOR /DME, the more the better. It generally takes more than one approach to get one's confidence renewed, so try to get approval to shoot the ILS to minimums, pull up straight ahead to fly out the back course, make the procedure turn to do the back course approach, then proceed out the front course for another trip down the glideslope. Repeat as needed, but don't quit on ILS approaches. Go over to a smaller field with a VOR circling approach, and put some precision into your non-precision approaches.

No-Radar Procedures

One byproduct of these boondocks approaches is that you may get some experience in a non-radar environment, rather a shock after being nestled comfortably in the lap of center radar. "Radar service terminated" comes as a rude awakening. A clearance to hold and "Expect further clearance at . . ." means another airplane is out there somewhere. With poor radar and communications coverage, arrangements have to be made for recontacting ATC after the missed approach. It's all good review for the rusty aviator sweating under his hood.

After making an abeam passage of the VOR out bound despite one's best efforts, one resolves to do better on the inbound. The procedure turn can be interesting with a bit of wind, and this knowledge had best be incorporated into the planning for timing the approach, anticipating a tailwind or headwind while coming down to the MDA. If, like many pilots, you steam along outbound at full cruise, then slow to an approach speed during the procedure turn, you will wait and wonder just when that approach fix is going to come up. Finally, it comes; you bomb down to MDA quickly in order to break out before reaching the one-mile circling radius, and struggle to hold MDA precisely while the time runs out. Don't forget to sing out on Unicom or 122.9 and keep your safety pilot awake; don't bust through a traffic pattern needlessly; pull up for the miss before penetrating the touch-and-go pattern if at all possible.

ADF approaches are equally fun, sometimes bordering on the mirthful before you begin to wonder what you would have done if the weather had been IMC and you missed the final approach course by two or three miles as you did today. Pin down a wind correction angle inbound on the initial approach and outbound for the procedure turn, then try to adjust your turn legs to bring you out onto the final approach course with the proper relative bearing to hold the course. Lotsa luck, and remember that this could be the only approach available someday.

The Failure Mode

Don't use your autopilot excessively; it's all right to practice its operation, but you should never knowingly place yourself in a position of needing the autopilot to get through a situation you couldn't handle on your own. It's a wise practice to simulate some equipment failures now and then, just to see what disruption it might cause in your routine. You never know how much you'll miss that second nav head until it goes bananas in the clouds. Partial panel work also deserves attention, against the day a gyro or vacuum pump goes to sleep.

Bringing yourself back to full currency is not just a matter of flying straight and level down the airway with the hood on; it's giving yourself a realistic workout. Plan on flying 1½ to 2 hours of approaches, as well as a little enroute work. By doing so, you will probably discover some shortcomings, and learn that currency is a relative thing. A legal logbook does not mean 200-and-one-half approaches are wise for you; set reasonable minimums above the legal ones, at least until you have regained full IFR proficiency.

Making yourself legally current can be either productive time well spent or a mere exercise in order to satisfy the FARs. Because your life and those of others in the IFR system may depend on your proficiency, resolve to gain and maintain all possible skills, not to just go through the motions. With time and practice, you can once again be a good instrument pilot.

Chapter 45

The Multi-Engine Rating

A multi-engine rating is one of the easiest and most popular additions to a pilot certificate. After the checkride, new multi-engine graduates delight in telling their envious single-engine buddies how painless it was and what a gas it is to fly big airplanes with two engines (probably a huge Piper Seminole).

While it is true that most experienced single-engine pilots can complete the multi-engine transition training with a minimum of fuss, the matter of competence shouldn't be taken lightly. Because operating costs of light twins are several times those of a Cessna 152, every effort is made to turn out a rated pilot in a minimum of air time. After all, just 10 hours of twin-engine dual instruction can cost half the price of a private ticket. All of which tends to make for legal—but barely competent—new multi-engine pilots. The operators' insurance companies know this, and in most cases the FBO can't rent multi-engine airplanes to his own graduates until they somehow acquire 25 hours or more of multi-engine time in their logbooks.

The shortest road to a safe twin transition starts on the ground; book learning is essential to safe operation and is more cost-effective than time spent in the cockpit. Several hours of study are required for each precious hour in the air. For your pocketbook's and your widow's sake, all the facts shouldn't be learned behind the wheel.

Are Twins Safer?

But why all this talk of accidents and careful training? Aren't two engines supposed to be safer than one? They are, but only in the hands of a properly trained pilot. Nearly all twin-engined aircraft are complex, heavy machines. They move fast and require their pilots to think a bit faster than they move. Like helicopters, twins can safely expand a pilot's field of operation *when operated within specific limitations*. Learning how to define these limitations is one of the main points of multi-engine training.

It is best to approach multi-engine transition after a background of flying in high-performance airplanes, gaining familiarization with retractable landing gear and controllable propellers, as well as with the slow-speed handling of a heavily laden wing.

Even before setting foot in the twin-engine aircraft it is ground school time. To understand how to operate with a twin's limitations you must learn why the twin has limitations in the first place. The study must include theory of twin-engine aerodynamics, normally in terms of conventional twins with wing-mounted engines turning clockwise as seen from the rear. Centerline-thrust twins, such as Cessna's Skymaster, are a simpler breed, and twins with the right engine turning counterclockwise, such as Piper's Seneca, are also special cases.

Basic Twin Theory

With both engines running, a twin is just another airplane, albeit a heavy, complex one. When one engine's power is lost and the aircraft is forced to carry on with the remaining thrust—ah, *that's* when things get interesting. In these circumstances it becomes a very poor flying machine indeed, even deadly if not managed properly. If density altitude is too high, the remaining engine's available horsepower may not be sufficient to maintain level flight, particularly with the aircraft in takeoff or landing configuration.

Here's why: Suppose, just to make it simple, that a certain aircraft needs 200 horsepower to maintain level flight in its minimum-drag condition. With two 250-horsepower engines, this means 300 excess horsepower are available to produce a zippy climb rate or fast cruise. Cage one engine, however, and only 50 horsepower will be available, and only under the best of conditions will the airplane be capable of climbing. The quoted single-engine service ceiling of the twin assumes a "clean" airplane (gear and flaps up) with the dead engine feathered and standard atmospheric conditions. At less than gross weight it may be bettered a bit, but it won't be approachable with everything hanging down, particularly when going around at a high-altitude airport. Under these conditions, when one engine fails, the twin merely becomes a noisy glider.

The windmilling prop produces a tremendous amount of drag when an engine is lost. Healthy amounts of rudder displacement are required to maintain straight flight at slow speeds and, as speed

Fig. 45-1. The sight of a feathered propeller means increased workload and quick decisions for the pilot. The multi-engine airplane MAY have enough performance to continue in level flight, or it may only have extended gliding range under some conditions.

decreases, a point is reached at which a turn into the dead engine will start despite full rudder to the contrary. The speed where this loss of control occurs is the dreaded V_{mc} or velocity of minimum control. The V_{mc} is highest at lower density altitudes, and many training demonstrations were conducted at insufficient altitude to recover when the airplane became unmanageable, with tragic results. There is no point in conducting V_{mc} demonstrations beyond the moment that a roll or turn begins. Certainly plenty of altitude—3000 feet or more—should be under the aircraft when investigating V_{mc}. If the demonstration is prolonged the aircraft may stall, which means a spin is probable, and twins aren't even designed to spin on two engines, much less one.

Much discussion centers about the "critical engine." This refers to the engine the pilot would *least* want to lose, as performance is poorer with this engine shut down than with its opposite number. The left engine is normally the critical engine in American-designed airplanes. The reason for the right engine's poorer showing is P-factor, which causes an airplane to yaw left in a climb unless right rudder is applied. At high angles of attack the propeller disc is tilted to the onrushing air. The descending blade, on the right-hand side of the disc as viewed from behind, is operating at a higher angle of attack as it turns than the ascending blade on the left. Thus the right-hand blade produces greater thrust. The effective center of the prop's thrust is no longer at the crankshaft, but moves to the right side of the propeller disc. This produces the yaw moment called P-factor, particularly significant in twins.

The Twin's V-Speeds

On a twin, the lowest V_{mc} speed is limited by the rudder control available to combat the yaw of single-engine flight. Because the center of thrust from a propeller operating at low airspeeds is displaced to the right, it follows that yaw from the right engine's asymmetrical thrust is made even worse by the P-factor. The left engine's yaw, on the other hand, is lessened by the P-factor shifting thrust to the inboard, rather than the outboard, side of the propeller disc. Thus, all other things being equal, the airplane will fly with less drag and down to a lower V_{mc} on the left engine, making it the critical one to lose. Piper's Seneca and Cessna's Crusader, for example, are fitted with counter-rotating engines in order to place P-factor inboard regardless of which engine loses power. This allows a lower certificated V_{mc} than would otherwise be possible.

Other speeds must be added to the stall and climb speeds a student normally learns in single-engine training. V_{mc} is one, of course, but that speed guarantees only *control,* not continued level flight or climb or even the ability to accelerate. Going on up the scale, one finds the best single-engine angle-of-climb speed, or V_{xse} for short. Holding this speed will bring the steepest possible climb, assuming the airplane has been cleaned up. Best rate-of-climb on one engine, or V_{yse} is a bit faster and offers a flatter climb but a greater rate of ascent. So to achieve true twin-engine safety you must not let the airplane leave the ground before V_{mc} is reached, and ideally the twin should have a long enough runway to accelerate almost up to V_{xse}, lose an engine, and still stop on pavement. This is the reason twin-engine pilots prefer long runways—not because the airplanes require extra length for the takeoff run, but because it is safer in case engine failure on takeoff makes a stop necessary. On short runways, a twin is frequently seen to consume almost the entire paved length before liftoff. "Boy, he barely made it!" exclaims the shocked onlooker. This isn't the case at all. The airplane was capable of flying long before the liftoff point, but the pilot wished to accelerate in low-drag profile until V_{mc} or V_{xse} was achieved.

Finally, We Fly

After doing enough ground study to make expensive airborne

training useful, it's time to go flying. Preflighting a twin offers no surprises beyond the obvious dual powerplants and, usually, a more complex fuel system with more sumps to drain. On board the aircraft, a few minutes should be spent in reviewing the cockpit layout before starting the engines. A multi-engine cockpit is "busier" than that of a lighter single-engine airplane, so it's wise to climb in and just sit for a while. Take the operator's manual home and sleep with it. It will probably be thicker and tougher than any you have digested so far in your career, and there is no substitute for knowing the aircraft—especially a new, challenging twin.

Expect to use a checklist in every twin to avoid overlooking a vital assessment or manipulation in proper sequence. Clear the area around the propellers carefully—especially the right prop, which may be difficult to see—before starting the engines. With both engines running and all systems "Go," the aircraft is ready to taxi. The amount of power needed to initially move the heavier airplane may be surprising. New twin pilots like to play inboard and outboard throttles to aid in making taxi turns, but it isn't necessary to carry this to extremes. With nosewheel steering, differential power isn't really needed; generally, retarding throttle on the inside of the turn is the best procedure, rather than "blasting" outside throttle.

After the runup checklist is completed, the takeoff must be met with a bit more planning than in single-engine airplanes. Remember, your concern is not so much for speed necessary to get the airplane off the ground as it is for the capability to continue flight if an engine fails. V_{mc} is marked by a red line on the airspeed indicator in newer twins, and V_{yse} is shown by a blue line. Ideally, you should leave the nosewheel on the runway until passing V_{mc} and plan to lift off around V_{xse}, which is just below V_{yse}. If an engine fails before the aircraft reaches V_{mc}, chop the throttles and stop. If an engine is lost after passing through V_{mc} stop if at all possible, but you may opt to hold V_{xse} carefully and clean up the airplane in an effort to make it fly. Speed in raising the gear and flaps and feathering the propeller on the dead engine is most important because the airplane will likely lose altitude at V_{xse} until the drag is lessened. In any event, do not permit airspeed to drift below V_{mc} during this phase, because, should you do so, full control would no longer be available.

So the twin is lined up for takeoff and the throttles are eased in smoothly. This time everything keeps running and the aircraft proceeds skyward for a little airwork. The first hour or so of dual will be spent primarily in learning to fly the airplane with both engines operating, through slow-flight, stalls, and other maneuvers. In later flights, single-engine drill will be learned until procedures become second nature.

When Two Become One

When one engine fails, your first job is to control the sudden yaw of the airplane into the dead engine. Normal use of rudder and aileron will hold the bird straight, but the pressure may be heavy—the student multi-engine pilot can expect a little soreness in his leg muscles after a good single-engine workout. While holding the airplane straight, maximum power is applied and steps are taken to clean up the airplane. This means all power controls are usually shoved full forward, without regard to engine gauges for the moment, and gear and flap controls are placed in the "Up" position. This procedure helps the airplane hold its altitude for a few seconds until you can feather the windmilling prop.

Identification of the dead engine comes next—and it's vital to be *absolutely* right. First, which foot is not holding rudder pressure? The dead foot is the dead engine, according to the time-honored cliche of twin training, and it works. The pilot who's holding hard right rudder *knows* his airplane's left engine is out, but just to be sure, he'll ease back the left throttle and see if engine noise and yaw remain unchanged. They do, so the dead engine has been identified. Now the prop control is moved back into "Feather" position and the dead engine's mixture control goes rearward to "Cutoff." Now the airplane will climb if density altitude and loading permit, assuming the busy pilot is still hanging onto V_{yse}. Using a 5° bank into the good engine will ease the rudder pressure required for straight flight and reduce drag to assist climb somewhat. Mags, generator, and fuel valve related to the dead engine are carefully turned off at this point.

Having learned to control the twin after losing an engine, and how to make a prompt—but not mechanical—shutdown of the windmilling engine, the rest of the training will seek to polish those skills in simulated emergency situations, such as losing an engine just after going around from a balked landing. At cruise speed an engine failure is no urgent catastrophe, but in full-dirty go-around configuration, survival depends on fast and correct handling of the situation.

Initial practice of emergency procedure is carried out at altitude, where full shutdowns to feather can be safely attempted. Then the training moves down into the traffic pattern for the real thing. There is no substitute for the feel of terra firma rushing by right under your hip pockets. Often a student who is cool and collected at altitude forgets everything he has learned when he sees the asphalt coming up at him at a great rate of speed. Naturally, low-altitude engine failures are only simulated. Instead of allowing the engine to be feathered, the instructor sets up 10 inches or so of manifold pressure—"Zero-thrust"—so power can be instantly restored should the need arise.

Ten hours of dual instruction is an average twin-engine transition time for a very competent pilot, although some have earned the rating in less. No written test is required, but the oral exam is thorough, as the examiner makes sure the candidate has done his homework. Do exactly as you have been taught during the inflight portion of the checkride and, presto, you will be a many-motor driver. If you are instrumented-rated, you will have to prove your ability to handle an engine failure and make an approach with the hood on. As stated earlier, your changes of going out and renting a twin right off are practically nil, so seek every chance to fly copilot or resign yourself to additional dual instruction. If you are fortunate enough to get to fly a twin regularly, make sure you ride at least annually with a competent multi-engine instructor to keep sharp on procedures rarely practiced after training. You'll enjoy every minute behind those twin throttles!

Chapter 46

The ATP: Aviation's Doctorate

According to the popular joke sheet found on flight school bulletin boards, Airline Transport Pilots are able to leap tall buildings at a single bound, walk on water, and generally excel at all sorts of challenging endeavors. This is not exactly untrue; ATPs can leap tall buildings with the aid of a Boeing 727 and have been known to walk on the water of a frozen hockey rink. In reality, ATPs are just competent professional pilots who have undergone a disciplined course of training to achieve the highest pilot rating bestowed by the FAA.

What's an ATP, Anyway?

The Airline Transport Pilot is prhaps the least-understood pilot rating. It carries only a few extra benefits beyond those of a commercial pilot certificate with an instrument rating, the primary one being the dubious privilege of giving "Instruction in Air Commerce." Because the ATP written and flight tests demand a high degree of knowledge and skill, the rating also has become a hiring requirement for most serious flying jobs, which is the reason it is sought by eager young pilots.

If two equally experienced pilots were to apply for a job, the ATP would probably get the nod over a mere commercial-instrument pilot. Commuter airline captains are now required to be ATP-rated, as is the pilot-in-command of an air taxi powered by jet engines or having 11 or more passenger seats.

The ATP originally was promulgated as an upgrade rating awarded to airline copilots moving over to the captain's seat. The applicant would be backgrounded in enroute and approach procedures, a current instrument pilot, and thoroughly familiarized with the aircraft's systems by flight engineer training or a transition school. In air carrier training programs, much of the checkride can be performed in a sophisticated simulator.

Going After It on Your Own

Individual pursuit of the ATP, a popular pastime with aspiring airline hopefuls, can be undertaken in as structured a manner as desired. Just about any twin-engine airplane up through bizjets can be used for the checkride, and no actual dual need by logged in preparation. However, it would be foolish to attempt the flight test without getting a lot of practice with an ATP in the right seat, preferably one who is also a practicing multi-engine CFI. A formal flight school is always best, especially since the FAA now allows certain designated examiners from these schools to give the ATP checkride, in addition to their inspectors. A typical 30-flight-hour /40-ground-school-hour ATP training course costs nearly half the price of a good automobile, however, and the rating can also be won by simply taking the flight test guide seriously and practicing in a familiar cockpit.

Basic requirements for the ATP include 1500 hours of pilot time, of which 500 hours must be cross-country flying, 100 hours night time, and at least 75 hours instrument flying. Unlike the preparation for other ratings, the ATP written may not be taken until the applicant has accumulated the required hours and passed his or her first-class medical exam. Both the logbook and medical certificate must be presented for inspection in order to take the written. No recommendation is necessary to take the written or flight tests, however. Evidently the pilot is supposed to know when he or she is ready, perhaps seeking the counsel of an ATP before making application.

Fig. 46-1. The sight of a Boeing 727 touching down brings out the pilot fever in everyone. At the controls is an ATP (airline transport pilot), the highest rating awarded by the FAA.

There is a choice of two written exams, one airline-oriented and requiring a thorough knowledge of Part 121 of the Federal Aviation Regulations, high-altitude meteorology, and the day-to-day operation of such airplanes as the Boeing 727, and the other commuter-airline oriented, covering a typical light turboprop flown under FAR Part 135. Achieving a passing score on such a test may not be of much practical value in general aviation flying, but it does prove that the individual can absorb an amazing amount of trivia if required. The exam consists of 80 multiple-choice questions in the style of all FAA writtens, with a six-hour time limit.

The oral portion of the flight test is designed to reveal the applicant's knowledge of his airplane's systems and limitations. The pilot's operating handbook must be memorized, for all practical purposes. Page-by-page explanation may be required, with "what if" questions posed at various points. Performance, loading, flight planning—all must be discussed in detail to the inspector's satisfaction before entering the airplane. A thorough preflight inspection is made, during which the applicant is expected to know the function and terminology for each item checked.

The Flight Test

The ATP flight test, by comparison, is nothing more than a highly critical instrument competency check taken in a high-performance airplane. While there is a single-engine ATP rating, as well as a helicopter ATP certificate, the multi-engine ATP is the usual working ticket sought for employment purposes. The ATP flight test guide, AC 61-77, lays it all out—each required maneuver, its desired objectives, and acceptable performance. The criterion is generally a commercial-pilot level of competence delivered despite such diversions as powerplant failures or equipment malfunctions. Altitude limits are generally plus-or-minus 100 feet, heading errors must be limited to 10°, and airspeed parameters are normally 10 mph. These are not overly generous margins in a high-performance airplane, and the task is often complicated by the need to control speed, altitude, and heading simultaneously, a skill seldom required for lesser ratings.

The acceptable-performance window narrows somewhat during critical moments, as during an instrument approach. MDA tolerance is plus 50 feet, minus zero, for example—not an easy target in low-level turbulence while running out the estimated time to the airport. The circle-to-land maneuver must be completed within the appropriate minimum-visibility radius without exceeding a 30° bank angle, and altitude tolerances are 100 feet above MDA, zero feet below. The manual ILS is to be flown with precision befitting a coupled autopilot, not more than one dot deviation right down to the DH while maintaining airspeed within 10 knots. Two types of non-precision approach must be demonstrated in addition to the ILS.

Engine-out emergencies are almost routine during an ATP checkride. The applicant is expected to maintain control and continue with the appropriate maneuver—be it a takeoff, ILS approach, or missed-approach procedure—while securing a failed engine. Tolerances for error are unchanged with an engine out; the same one-dot deviation on the ILS and 10-knot airspeed control must be maintained. A thorough knowledge of cockpit controls is vital at this time.

The aspiring ATP should expect a heavy workload during the flight check; instruction and practice will emphasize this. One ATP checkride of my acquaintance required a manual landing gear extension during single-engine holding at an NDB, as an example. Flying the aircraft with precision must be almost second nature, allowing part of one's attention to be directed elsewhere—beating out flames or whatever. Quite simply, the ATP is expected to be able to cope with any conceivable emergency at any moment, ensuring the survival of his passengers under the most adverse conditions. It is a serious rating—attainable by anyone willing to undergo stringent preparation but not easily obtained with a week's practice.

If you feel an ATP rating would improve your self-esteem, total up your hours, take a first-class flight physical, and get a written exam study guide or enroll in a ground-school course. The written results are good for two years, giving ample time to practice for the flight test. If you're really serious about precision flying, you can join the ranks of airline transport pilots and learn to walk on water yourself.

Index

Hotstarts, 95